ENERGY

52 ways to fire up your life
and become an energy angel

Jo Salter & Daniel Summer

© Copyright 2006 Jo Salter & Daniel Summer.
All rights reserved. No part of this publication may be reproduced, stored in a retrieval system, or transmitted, in any form or by any means, electronic, mechanical, photocopying, recording, or otherwise, without the written prior permission of the author.

Note for Librarians: A cataloguing record for this book is available from Library and Archives Canada at www.collectionscanada.ca/amicus/index-e.html
ISBN 1-4120-8446-6

Printed in Victoria, BC, Canada. Printed on paper with minimum 30% recycled fibre. Trafford's print shop runs on "green energy" from solar, wind and other environmentally-friendly power sources.

TRAFFORD
PUBLISHING™
Offices in Canada, USA, Ireland and UK

Forma Publishing in association with Trafford Publishing.

Book sales for North America and international:
Trafford Publishing, 6E–2333 Government St.,
Victoria, BC V8T 4P4 CANADA
phone 250 383 6864 (toll-free 1 888 232 4444)
fax 250 383 6804; email to orders@trafford.com

Book sales in Europe:
Trafford Publishing (UK) Limited, 9 Park End Street, 2nd Floor
Oxford, UK OX1 1HH UNITED KINGDOM
phone 44 (0)1865 722 113 (local rate 0845 230 9601)
facsimile 44 (0)1865 722 868; info.uk@trafford.com

Order online at:
trafford.com/06-0201

10 9 8 7 6 5 4 3

For our children,

who teach us more about energy every day.

Contents

5 **Introduction**

7 Part 1 **Energise Your Mind and Your Body Will Follow**

35 Part 2 **The Dead Don't Fail**

47 Part 3 **Energy Vampires**

67 Part 4 **React or Respond?**

93 Part 5 **Energy Angels**

107 Part 6 **Universal Energy**

141 Part 7 **Rock Your World!**

Introduction

This book is about your personal energy and how to store it, boost it and use it. If we had to use one word, we'd say this book is about your *zingzip!*

So what makes this book different? Well, we believe that personal energy is as individual as you are. Where other books prescribe running faster and lifting weights, we ask you to use the power of your own mind. Instead of bullying you into starvation with the latest fad diet, we ask you to look within and discover what your body really needs.

Think of your mind as your most powerful muscle. We are going to show you how to harness its power so that you improve and excel in every area–not just physical energy, but emotional and intellectual energy too.

You are the real subject of this book. You create energy and consume energy; you give energy a form—your mind and body are its channels and containers. It's you who converts energy into events that change the world, or small delightful happenings appreciated only by a few.

Particular qualities of energy change the quality of life, and we can change the way we create, consume and use energy to power our dreams, our every-day lives and even our spiritual adventures.

Energy is everywhere! Live it, love it, burn it! Store it up — then spend it. Give it away or amplify it! You can even zingzip it! It's your life-blood, the song you sing when you're alone, and the dreams you have for yourself and others. *It's your life!*

How To Use This Book

The book is divided into seven sections and fifty two chapters. We like to think that you will read it cover to cover, then come back to each chapter and try out the ideas and practical exercises for one whole week. In this way, the change in your energy can really make a difference, and you can keep up the fun of increasing your energy, health and happiness for the whole year.

PART 1

✳

Energise Your Mind and Your Body Will Follow

This art of resting the mind and the power of dismissing from it all care and worry is probably one of the secrets of energy in our great men.

Captain J.A. Hadfield

Imagine that everything in the universe is connected. Everything around you is interacting with everything else, as different energies assume one dynamic form after another.

You can see this connectedness and energy in the weather. As rain falls onto hills and mountains, first streams, then great rivers are formed, irrigating the land to bring new forms of life from the earth, then tumbling into the oceans. Condensation causes water vapour to rise, and rain-bearing clouds once more form above the land and sea. And so the cycle continues.

The interconnectedness of life, and the energy that sustains it, can be seen in the way that we breathe. Through the processes of inspiration and expiration the air is filtered, your lungs extract the oxygen needed for healthy blood and other vital functions, and carbon dioxide is expired. Plants and the sun then combine through photosynthesis to produce oxygen. Plants breathe. Humans breathe. The sun shines. Rain falls. It is all connected.

Life as we know it couldn't continue if any single part of the system was removed. It's a beautiful, indivisible living whole, although science continues to work on breaking the life force down into ever smaller parts.

Some of these life-functions work on the cellular level. Others need electron microscopes to observe changes that can only be understood at the molecular level. Physicists observe smaller and smaller particles, until it becomes obvious that what's being observed can no longer even be described as a particle. At the root of everything, there's only energy.

For centuries, there's been a debate about the mind and the body, and whether they are separate entities. But the evidence has mounted that, just like the sun and rain, the human breath and the breath of plants, the mind and body are indivisible.

The mind guides the body to seek food, shelter and rest. In pre-modern societies, seeking food took care of exercise. Now, especially in the overweight western hemisphere, seeking food doesn't consume a fraction of the calories contained in the food we eat, and the way we get it doesn't develop muscles, strengthen bones, or improve stamina. Modern life gives us too much food, of too little quality, for too little effort.

The human mind-body system is unique. Searching for food, finding shelter and resting are common to all animals. What's different about the human condition is that we have a highly developed consciousness. Deliberate steps can be taken to improve health, fitness and well-being. The connection between our minds and bodies is so strong that the mind can be used to improve the well-being of the body, and vice-versa.

Energy is simply the stuff you use to power your mind and body. You can achieve a natural balance that will help you to be fitter, happier, calmer and wiser.

Energy is more than just food calories. It underlies all of life, our bodies, thoughts and dreams. The Chinese call it chi, and if it helps, you can call it spirit. But whatever it is, let's get on with finding out how to get more of it!

Chapter 1
Look after your body

> *Keeping your body healthy is an expression of gratitude to the whole cosmos - the trees, the clouds, everything.*
> THICH NHAT HANH

A healthy body is a marvellous thing — as long as being healthy doesn't become an unhealthy obsession. Energy flows best in a balanced system, and an unfit body is a system out of balance. This chapter is a quick review of some of the basics of getting mind and body energy flowing together powerfully.

A healthy body will channel energy through itself — it will keep the mind clear, the spirits soaring and the senses keen.

On the other hand, you can choose to eat too much, to smoke and be sedentary, and still live to be a hundred. Many great thinkers and wits (such as Mark Twain) have advised that course of action. They argue that to deprive the body of what it wants for the sake of health is mean-spirited and self-defeating. Some people may even live to be a hundred with a reasonable quality of life. Others just don't want to live that long!

For most people, this just isn't the case. If we treat our bodies badly, we suffer.

Mental or physical suffering is what happens when you can't use the energy which is all around. Suffering stops you from achieving your goals and doing what you really enjoy. It saps your energy.

Optimal health needs optimal energy. There are some underlying principles that can help you to keep your body healthy and energetic.

So getting healthy starts right now!

Make this your mission: start looking now for a system of exercise that fulfils as many of the following as possible:

- ✔ Strengthens bones and muscle (yoga; weight training)
- ✔ Improves flexibility (yoga; chi-kung)
- ✔ Improves balance (yoga; tai-chi chuan)
- ✔ Focuses on the mind-body connection (yoga; tai-chi, chi-kung)
- ✔ Improves the cardio-vascular system (any activity you enjoy that increases heart rate: jogging; dancing; football)

The key to energy is action. The idea of *motivation* has its roots in 'motivare' — to move towards. So physical movement is essential, and will help us to move in other ways — spiritually and intellectually. When you think of *motivating yourself* — physically move towards whatever it is that you want. For instance — you see an attractive man or woman that you would like to know better. Time is short, perhaps you're at a party and will never see this person again. Do you really think you can make a connection with this person by moving away from them, or keeping your distance? *Move towards whatever it is that you want in your life.*

Energy is also connected with food, of course. Food is part of the complex system that allows energy to flow through the body and to be used efficiently and creatively. Again there are simple principles that if followed will make you look and feel energised and healthy.

- ✔ Learn to recognise your own hunger
- ✔ Only eat when hungry
- ✔ Don't overload your digestive system
- ✔ Eat a wide variety of foods, including plenty of fruits and vegetables
- ✔ Enjoy food, and think about its effects on your body

The last point is important for people who are struggling to maintain a healthy diet. With a little will-power, you can pause just for a moment before eating, and think about what you are putting into your body. Will its effect be to energise you, and make you feel powerful and light? Or will it make you feel leaden: devoid of energy, slow and heavy?

Start to be aware of the effect that the mind and your attitudes have on your weight and health. Increasing numbers of researchers in the field of well-being are confirming that attitudes really do affect health.

- ✔ Conscious *optimism* helps stave off both 'low moods' and minor illnesses
- ✔ Stress controlling techniques such as *meditation* increase resistance to disease
- ✔ *Visualise* energy coursing through your mind and body. This can actually help to repair minor damage and have other remarkable physical and mental effects
- ✔ A positive *intention* to be healthy can aid quicker recovery from illness
- ✔ Tell yourself you have *energy*-visualise it in your muscles, your bones, and coursing through your blood. This can have a remarkable effect!

We'll come back to some of these themes in the course of the book. In the meantime, *think and get healthy!*

Chapter 2
Spend a day on yourself (better yet, a week!)

Ask anyone—there is more stress today than ever before. And yet people of working age today go about their daily tasks in unprecedented luxury compared to days gone past. There are still accidents and unacceptable working conditions, but in general manual labour is less dangerous than it has ever been. Workers are better protected by their unions, the laws, and their own heightened awareness of safety. White collar workers for the most part spend their days in comfortable, well heated offices, while many drivers sit in air conditioned luxury, listening to music as they go from one job to the next, or from home to work.

And yet... many feel that they are somehow on a treadmill that's physically, mentally and spiritually exhausting.

In the midst of affluence that past generations could only dream of, many people live through an internal nightmare of insecurity and fear. Some respond to these pressures with aggression or breakdown. Road rage is the mental illness of the day.

Meanwhile, the traditional roles of the sexes are broken down, for better or worse. Women building homes, paying for them and fixing them, cooking in them, and raising children in them. Men working every hour to hold everything together, to keep one step ahead, not daring to look over their shoulders at whatever it is that keeps them running.

It's time to stop.
Take a deep breath.
Take a day off.

If you're devoid of energy, running out of whatever juice it is that you need to keep you going, then take a day off. Not just from your job. Not even just from your husband or wife, your kids and the dog. Take a day off from your life. A week if you can manage it.

So what are you going to do with this gift of a day, a day that is for you and you alone? Well, here are some things that you *could* do —

- ✔ You could listen to a Philip Glass CD — North Star, maybe — and get lost in the beauty of the patterns it forms in your head
- ✔ You could go to a day spa and be pampered and massaged and oiled
- ✔ You could visit a fine museum and get into the visions of artists from different civilisations, past and present
- ✔ You could walk in nature and appreciate the beauty all around us

These things will help to replenish your vitality and lift the spirits. They are heartily recommended. But all of these things, no matter how refreshing and invigorating they are at the time, will fade and vanish all too quickly. If you gave yourself a Friday off and did all or some or one of these activities, the effect might last until mid-way through Monday. So here's a more radical course of action.

Use this day off to review your life. Where are you now? How did you get here? Where are you going? How will you get *there*?

The unexamined life is not worth living.
Socrates (in Plato)

If you do this well, you'll gain more energy, purpose and drive than any number of spa days could ever give you. So how do you go about it?

The first two questions — "where am I now?" and "how did I get here" are the least important. To get to your ultimate destination, it isn't crucial for you to understand in detail how you got to be where you are now. It's a new day. To illustrate what we mean, imagine you are sailing around the Mediterranean. You're in port, maybe in Marseilles. But that is only really important when it comes to setting course for your next destination.

Maybe you ended up in Marseilles through a navigation error. You expected to be much further east in the Med by now, but were blown off course... You feel guilty about the fact that you ignored the weather bulletins. You blame yourself for the lack of progress.

None of that will get you anywhere. *Just be aware of where you are now.*

The really important part of this process is to understand where you want to get to, and what steps you must take to get there. If you want to understand the techniques that will help you to do that, go to Chapter 38 — *Energy and the path to your dreams* — right now. It contains everything you need to invent your own future and turn it into reality!

Chapter 3

Reduce your age today

Make today all about energy!

> *Youth is a quality, and if you have it, you never lose it*
> FRANK LLOYD WRIGHT

Carpe Diem — seize the day! And when tomorrow comes along — seize that too!

This is not about running around like an insane kid, or pasting a false smile on your face if inside you feel empty. Energy and youth are attitudes. They are things to be marshalled by your will, your desire and your sheer exuberance, your joy at being alive.

You may be thinking 'but I don't feel joy at being alive. I have problems. Lots of them. There's the rent and the…'

In that case, try a simple exercise that's in two parts. You really need to *do* this, not just read about it. It's time for you to participate.

Think about what it would feel like if you *were* full of joy at being alive. What would that feel like? What would you see? What would you taste and smell? How would others start to act towards you? Visualise what that would be like for you. Try it right now.

Do you think it's possible that others would act differently towards you, perhaps be happier around you, enjoy your company more, and seek you out more often? And what would it feel like to be *exuberant*? How would you look if you *were* full of vitality? Standing a little straighter, maybe, and breathing more easily? Is the act of thinking about these things, right now, already changing your physiology?

Remember, the mind and the body are an integral system. Work on the mind and the body will respond. If this first part of the exercise has worked for you and you are imagining being joyful, exuberant and powerful, then what's the difference between you and someone who actually *is* all of those things?

Perhaps the difference just disappeared.

Now for the second part of the exercise. ***For the next twenty four hours, act as though you are the age that you want to be.*** Pretend that you are absolutely full of joy and bursting with vitality. For the purposes of this game, imagine that nothing can get you down and you have all the energy needed to overcome any obstacle. You don't even have to believe it. Just act as if it is true. Come back tomorrow...

24 hours later

Did you 'pretend' all day? Did it work for you? If not, try again by imagining more vividly what it would be like to be the age you want to be. Imagine your feelings, how you would look and sound, and how you would move. Feel the joy, taste it, live it. If it did work, go back to the start and do it again!

Throughout this book we will emphasise that your attitudes and mode of thinking are the most important factors in energising your life. Youth is powered by your attitude towards it, and energy is what will make sure you keep as young as you want to be.

So why youth, anyway?

At its best, youth is full of *vitality*. It's *open* to new ideas and new ways of thinking, acting and being. Youth has a *spirit of adventure*. Youth lives in the moment, but has *joyful expectations of wonderful things in the future*.

You know what to do next. Ask yourself...

What would you feel like if you were full of vitality, were open to all kinds of new ways of doing things, had a fantastic spirit of adventure and knew that your life will be full of wonderful things?

Imagine it now. Feel it, smell it, taste and see it. Close your eyes and see the vital you, the way you walk, talk and go about the world. Now take that attitude, those thoughts and feelings, and act as if they were true. That's when the magic happens — because those things suddenly *are* true.

Enjoy your youth!

Chapter 4
Use the breath

You need to breathe. The processes involved in human respiration — such as the oxygenation of blood cells — are vital to keeping you alive. But there are more subtle uses of the breath and many ways in which it can energise you.

In Western culture, energy is often associated with the chemical reactions that take place during 'fight or flight' reactions. These aren't controlled by the conscious mind. Even when we use bursts of energy for things such as games or sports, we're simulating the basic primordial reaction to a threatening environment. Many sporting activities simulate flight (jogging and running) or fight (in overpowering an opponent in some way, as happens in most sports).

When athletes are in 'flow', they are harnessing their energies to maximum effect in breaking a record or defeating an opponent. When questioned after 'peak' or 'flow' experiences, athletes often observe that their minds had become calm, empty of all other considerations, the conscious mind barely used to help the performance. The athlete is using huge amounts of energy with an easy, relaxed, yet unbending will and purpose for which the conscious mind isn't needed. But it's the threat from the environment (or the opponent, or the record to be broken) that enables this process to happen.

What if you could use the mind to harness these enormous energies within us, without there first being a threat from the environment? Through the use of the breath and the mind, this is absolutely possible.

At first sight, it seems like the 'flow' experience of enormously enhanced energy also creates the side-effect of having a calm mind. But let's turn that on its head. Suppose that it's the calm mind itself that enables the peak state to happen! But before we delve into that, let's consider how energy, the mind and the breath are regarded in Eastern cultures.

In India, China and other Eastern countries, the breath is of vital importance in systems of exercise, meditation, mind control and energy generation. Energy runs through not only the human body, but the whole universe.

In traditional Chinese medicine and philosophy in particular, the health of the body depends on maintaining an uninterrupted flow of energy. The role of medicine is to remove blockages. It's also thought that energy can be taken in from the world around us, and that simply by being alive we are involved in a 'Chi' or energy exchange with the Universe. This is like the connection between the breath of humans, the respiration of trees and the rest of nature, as we mentioned earlier. The Chinese believe that trees, bushes, plants and the sun are particularly fine sources of energy, which is why they often exercise in parks and near trees.

It's possible to devote a life-time of study to understanding the various systems of breath control involved in Yoga, Chi Kung and Tai Chi. Let's get started right now with some simple breathing techniques that will help you to calm the mind and fill your whole being with energy.

You can use trial and error to memorise the following and put it into action, but it may be a good idea to have a trusted friend calmly and gently read the passage to you until such time as you memorise the technique.

Technique!

Energy Breathing

First of all, sit quietly in a place where you won't be disturbed. Place your feet flat on the floor, your hands comfortably in your lap, and close your eyes. Breathe gently and without strain through your nostrils. Be aware of the air as it enters and exits your body.

Now follow the air downwards into your lungs. Do not strain, hold the breath, or deliberately breathe more deeply. Simply be conscious of the breath and its journey into your body. Let any thoughts that arise simply fall away.

Let the mind follow the breath. Now breathe gently into an area which the Chinese call the Tan Tien. This is situated the width of three fingers below your navel, and about one third of the way into your body, starting from your belly, back towards your spine. Take the breath to that point. Relax. Breathe out. Continue.

Now, as you breathe in, allow your mind to travel with the breath. Experience the breath as life–giving energy. Feel the energy flowing into the Tan Tien. Give the energy a colour—perhaps gold, like the life–giving sun.

As you breathe out, imagine the energy that you absorbed flowing out not just with the breath through your nostrils, but also through your hands, feet, the top of your head, and anywhere else that you feel will energise you. Feel the power of breath, of your mind, and of the life–force. Visualise the golden rays of energy bursting from you. When you're ready,

gently bring your mind back to the room in which you're sitting, and carry the energy from inside back out into the world.

Do this exercise often. Perfect the technique. It's a great basis for many of the other techniques you will find in the rest of the book. You can find more on the breath and getting energy from nature in Part 6 – "Tapping into Universal Energy".

Chapter 5
Mantras for maximum energy and well-being

Now that you know how to quiet the mind and use that state of calmness to generate feelings of well-being and energy, here's another technique to help you carry this feeling through the day.

Be open-minded. Perhaps you find it hard to believe, for example, that it's possible to attract good things into your life, simply by focusing your attention on them. It's healthy to be sceptical — in fact, with so many false gurus and charlatans around, it can be downright essential. Just be aware that there's no advice given in this book which has not been validated by the personal experience of the authors. So give these things a try! You have nothing to lose, and masses to gain.

This is a really powerful technique. Try it when you know you'll have a quiet day. As you become more skilled and experienced, you'll be able to use it in the midst of all kinds of craziness. It will help to keep you happy, healthy and aligned with Universal Energy.

Technique!
Mantra for Health, Happiness and Energy

Breathe in through your nostrils, as demonstrated in the 'Energy Breathing' technique. Let any thoughts that arise simply fall away.

Breathe in as you silently say to yourself, with great calmness, and assurance

I am healthy
Breathe out.
Breathe in as you calmly say to yourself

I am happy
Breathe out.
Breathe in as you gently say to yourself

I give energy
Breathe out.
Breathe in as you gratefully say to yourself

I receive energy
Breathe out.
Continue the breath / mantra cycle

I am healthy

I am happy

I give energy

I receive energy

You'll soon see that you can physically move around as you do this. You can go out into the world, taking your mantra with you. You will find that the world changes with you and for you.

Health, happiness and energy. What more do you need?

Chapter 6
Fast for a day

> *Make hunger thy sauce,*
> *as a medicine for health.*
> THOMAS TUSSER, 1524

Here's an idea that you might want to try. It's not for everyone, and you should approach it carefully. But you could be someone who would really benefit from fasting for a day, and be rewarded with a huge dose of energy. How and why? Read on…

It's been said that the hardest working system in the human body is the digestive system. Many people give their guts huge amounts of work to do — day in, day out. The human body evolved when food supplies were far less predictable than they are for most people in the developed world. We eat and drink because we can — not because we need to, or even want to.

Every day, we're tempted by advertising for foods that increase several things about us — waistlines, weight, feelings of ill-health and cravings for yet more food. Many products are specifically designed to be 'more-ish', to encourage us to eat and keep on eating. Packed full of preservatives, colourings, additives and other chemicals, these foods may well be sending 'wellness' signals to the brain, because they stimulate our brains with their sweetness and saltiness — but our bodies are groaning under the strain.

The sheer bulk of what we eat, the processing of the chemicals involved, the huge efforts our bodies have to go through to purify what we put into them, and to convert the excess energy into stores of unwanted fat that we will never use — all of this takes huge amounts of energy! No wonder so many of us wake up after a night's sleep still feeling exhausted, lethargic and wrung out — our digestive systems have been working all night to clear the way for the next day's mountain of food!

Fasting is one way in which to occasionally call a halt to this madness — if for no other reason than to give our guts a rest. If you decide to fast, do so only for a maximum of twenty four hours. Make sure you drink lots of water, or even fresh fruit juices. You will be resting your digestive system and also, if you observe yourself carefully, you will be re-acquainted with your own hunger. This is a very important side effect. One thing you can take away from a day of fasting is that you'll be able to distinguish between craving a foodstuff, feeling peckish, and true hunger. True hunger is the body's genuine signal that it needs food to maintain optimum efficiency by eating. Don't panic when you hear this signal! It's an early warning sign — not a red alert telling you death through starvation is imminent!

Some people may experience headaches and even dizziness when they attempt to fast. If you are one of them, call a halt immediately and eat something healthy and fresh, such as fruit. Thankfully, there's another method of achieving the same boost of energy that has the added advantage that it can be used frequently.

Technique!
Eating for Energy

This technique uses hunger to control your intake of food. It should help you to dramatically reduce the amount of food you are asking your body to process. You can do it two or three days a week, and more if you feel yourself becoming healthier, stronger and more energetic.

First of all, listen out for the hunger signal. Be aware that the first one you get will probably be just a craving. Use will power! Fight your way through it! Or even better, deflect it gently by thinking about more important things!

The next signal will have a slightly different quality to it. You feel 'peckish'. You really want some food, and you are convinced that this is real hunger. Don't give up! This is an impostor – it probably isn't a true sign that you need to eat.

The next signal will be true hunger. Strangely enough, it is the easiest to ignore. You can somehow live with this feeling of true hunger more easily, and could carry on without food quite comfortably for a while. This is probably because the feelings aroused by true hunger are not meant to completely disable us. Our ancestors would have needed all their wits, strength and speed at this time to track down and harvest new sources of food.

Nevertheless, don't ignore the hunger signal – but don't go on a binge either. Try eating much smaller amounts than you normally would. Have natural, well balanced foods – fruits, nuts, good sources of protein and grains, for example – ready to help you ward off the hunger. These kinds of food

– particularly fruit and vegetables, which are water – rich – are easily digested.

Another tip is to chew each mouthful of food very thoroughly. This will aid in digestion and somehow seems to satisfy the hunger much more quickly. Stop as soon as you feel you have eaten enough.

You will be amazed at how much less food you eat on a day when you let hunger decide when and what you will eat. You will feel lighter, brighter and full of energy!

Chapter 7
Losing weight? It's just a game!

It's exhausting to carry around fat stores — if you're overweight, losing pounds will energise you more than any other single thing. You'll look better, feel better and be able to do more things that add to your energy stores — it's a virtuous circle. You'll also be less prone to all kinds of diseases, from heart problems to joint pain.

Although diet fads come and go, there are some things we can say with confidence about food, weight, and how to lose it:

- ✔ Weight gain is caused by consuming more calories than you expend. Calories are just a measure of the energy value of foods. If you consume on average 2600 calories a day, but only expend 2550, that small 50 calorie difference will result in 'creeping obesity' — slow weight gain over a fairly long period
- ✔ A healthy diet is a varied diet. You need fruits, vegetables, nuts, grains, cereals and lean protein (there are superb non–meat products available that are high in protein and low in fat, but for meat eaters, protein needs to be lean)
- ✔ Consume as few processed foods as possible, as these tend to be low in vitamins, fibre and protein, and high in fat, sugars, salt and chemicals
- ✔ Regular exercise not only expends more calories — it can also strengthen the bones, develop the muscles, improve flexibility, the cardio–vascular system, strength and stamina. By speeding up the metabolism, the fat-burning effects can continue for hours after your exercise session

If it's true that consuming only a small amount of calories more than the number you expend will eventually make you overweight, it's equally true that just a minor adjustment will lead to a decrease in weight. Eat a tiny bit less, exercise or be active a tiny bit more, stick at it—and you WILL lose weight. A good approach to this is to aim to lose just one pound a week. The adjustments needed to achieve this are really minimal.

A weight loss of one pound per week seems very slow to some people who want instant, visible results. But haven't we seen, time and again, that crash diets just don't work? If you deprive the body of what it needs, it will enter 'starvation mode', and lay up fat stores as best it can. If you push crash diets far enough, the body will start to consume its own muscle tissue as fuel, and you will get ill. Eventually, you'll have to take on large amounts of fuel to return the body to equilibrium, and you'll put back on any weight that you managed to lose.

So let's think about this one pound per week weight loss again. It seems a lot more attractive if we think about it this way: see yourself in thirty weeks time. You are thirty pounds lighter. You are healthier and fitter. You are not starving yourself, and you are free of food cravings. And all you have done is eat slightly less (perhaps changing the kinds of things you eat along the way for a healthier diet) and exercised slightly more.

If it were all that simple, there would be no diet industry, and the shelves of bookshops would not be groaning under the weight of the hundreds of diet books. There are many good books on weight loss out there (and even more crazy ones that probably do more harm than good). But the key to losing weight and gaining energy is all in the mind. And finding the key to what will help you stay on the right road to weight loss—that will help you to keep on eating slightly less and exercising slightly more—is in your own approach to life, and in the way that you think.

No single system of motivation will work for everyone—to a great extent only you can discover what works. But read on, and see if you think this might help. This method can be applied to anything you want to motivate yourself to do—from losing weight, to finding love, to making yourself a financial success. The idea is—*it's all just a game.*

First of all, we need to think about what makes a game a game, and we can break it down as follows, using the game of Chess as an example:

A game has
- ✔ An objective — e.g., to checkmate the opponent's King
- ✔ Rules — e.g., a Bishop may only move diagonally
- ✔ Tactics — e.g., don't move your own Queen too early
- ✔ Built-in penalties and rewards — e.g., advance a Pawn to your opponent's end of the board and reclaim a lost piece
- ✔ Equipment — e.g. chess pieces and board

So if weight loss was just a game, how would we play it? What follows is an example — you can adjust to your own requirements:

Technique!

The Weight Loss Game

Objective: Lose 28 pounds in 28 weeks
Starting weight on Monday of week one = 200 pounds
Target weight on Sunday of week 24 = 176 pounds

Rules: The player uses a graph to plot weight loss. The graph shows the ideal weight on any Monday. As each week passes, the player weighs—in and plots the actual weight on the graph. The aim is to stick as closely to the ideal weight as possible. If the player is over 3lbs more than the target weight, s/he has one week in which to get back on target. If the player is more than 3lbs less than the target weight, s/he is losing weight too quickly and has one week to get back on target.

> **Tactics:** The player will eat only when hungry. No processed foods will be eaten. Fruit and vegetables will be eaten every day. In addition, exercise will consist of using the stairs instead of the lift, stretching every day, getting off the bus a stop early, and taking a long walk every Saturday.
>
> **Penalties and Rewards:** Failure to keep to the target weight as described in the rules means that the game is over! If weight is on target, the following rewards are given:
>
> Week 7 (7 pounds lighter)—New Bicycle
> Week 14 (14 pounds lighter)—Book a walking holiday in the Pyrenees
> Week 21 (21 pounds lighter)—A day at a Spa
> Week 28 (28 pounds lighter)—Buy complete new wardrobe—you'll need one!
>
> Equipment: Scales for weighing. Graph paper. A pencil and ruler.

Notice that the rewards will actually accelerate the whole process of losing weight, gaining energy and improving health and well–being.

Enjoy the game!

PART 2

✣

The Dead Don't Fail

> Far better it is to dare mighty things, to win glorious triumphs even though checkered by failure, than to rank with those poor spirits who neither enjoy nor suffer much because they live in the gray twilight that knows neither victory nor defeat.
>
> **Theodore Roosevelt**

The only people who never fail are the people who never try. Failure means activity, and without it, no progress can be made. As Thomas J. Watson, the founder of IBM, once said:

> Would you like me to give you a formula for success?
> It's quite simple really
> **Double your rate of failure.**

Someone else once said, it isn't the fact that you got knocked down that makes you a failure, it's how long you stay down.

What is failure anyway? It's nothing more than a state of mind. You can't touch failure or smell it or see it. It's what is known as a nominalization—a noun that's been created from the verb to fail.

Failure has no reality in itself—it's a belief you have about your environment. So you can do two things about it—change your attitude or change your environment.

> *"Fear is a question: What are you afraid of, and why? Just as the seed of health is in illness, because illness contains information, your fears are a treasure house of self-knowledge if you explore them."*
> MARILYN FERGUSON

Failure is often associated with fear, which is another word that describes an internal state or attitude. But fear can be used in a very positive way. The adrenalin that pumps around the body when you're scared is made of the same chemicals that pump around your body when you're happy and excited. It's just a way that the body and the mind prepare us to act. So even fear can be seen as a friend.

Sometimes you might feel that you're failing in a long term sense—that you're doing the 'wrong' things with your life. Use this section to realign with the purpose that you knew you had in your formative years, or that's developed since, maybe as an interest or passion.

Follow your heart in what you do with the rest of your life, and there won't be any such thing as failure—only different ways to experience working at what you really love to do. That's the most energising activity of all.

> *Success is the ability to go from one failure to another with no loss of enthusiasm.*
> SIR WINSTON CHURCHILL
> (1874 - 1965)

Chapter 8
Do the work you love

Today, tell yourself that *there is only so much time.*

Sorry to break the news to you, but one day you're going to die!

Are you using your time wisely? Are you enjoying every ounce of love and life that you can? Don't put it off until tomorrow. Do it today. Do it now.

Every life has a pattern, but while you are immersed in your own life, it's hard to see what that pattern is. Imagine yourself at the end of your life, looking back. Realise that you can consciously change the pattern, and you can do it today. Maybe you will look back at this period of your life and think, *I chose the safe option, and God, it was boring!* Or perhaps you will see that this was the time when you decided to find your true purpose, to follow it with passion and enjoyment, and to contribute something to the world that made the pattern of your life full of subtle and profound meaning.

Someone once said that nobody's last words were ever *if only I'd spent more time at the office.*

Working life takes up a huge amount of the time we spend on earth. But that could be a positive statement, not a cause for regret. The biggest single waste of energy and the sheer joy of life is to be stuck in a job that you don't like, that pays the household bills but not the spiritual ones, that leaves your belly full and your mind and soul empty. It's a huge waste of energy to work at the things we don't like, just so we can accumulate more of the stuff that we don't really want.

So how can you get in touch with the things that you really like to do, and that might support you in putting a roof over your head? What would make your working life a source of strength, be so enjoyable and fulfilling that the boundary between work and play, or work and 'retirement' would become meaningless? There are some really useful questions you can ask yourself, and in the next chapter we'll focus on just one of them.

For now though, ask yourself this: **what did I really love as a child, and in my teenage years? What kind of future did I see for myself?**

Let Dan share his experience of this:

"When I was a kid, although I did my share of kicking footballs around and getting into scrapes, I was really an ideas person. I loved books — history, fiction, astronomy, tales of great explorers. I decided that I would be a writer. It seemed to me that there was no greater calling than to bring ideas into the world — ideas that would move and inspire people, and remind them of how beautiful life can be.

I was young. I thought time was endless for me, that there was no rush. Stuff happened — I needed a job. I still wrote a little, but the writing seemed not good enough and I began to lose confidence. Meanwhile, my job let me buy a few things. And those few things multiplied. Then I needed a car to drive to a better job to maintain the things I'd bought. I needed a nicer suit to work at that better job. I needed a bigger TV to help anaesthetize the aching soul that was being desiccated by that better job!

By now, writing for me was a kind of conversation piece: 'I like to write'. I thought it made me more interesting than to say 'I work at a job I don't like', although heaven knows I said that a lot too. The idea of bringing ideas and beauty into the world had been totally forgotten, lost under the weight of 'earning a living'.

And then one day, quite suddenly it seemed (although I suspect there was a long process involved), I woke up. I remember how it happened.

I was studying on a management course dealing with 'Change and Consulting in Organisations'. We were each encouraged to use pictures from magazines, or our own drawings, to create a collage of a pressing business or personal issue, a kind of picture of where things stand right now.

It was a powerful experience. I was able to express my fears and hopes and dreams from outside of spoken language. I used pictures, colours, strange juxtapositions that helped explain where I was, how I came to be here, and where I was going. I could access emotions that are usually suppressed by the conventions of normal speech.

To cut a long story short, I was able to see the pattern of my life thus far. I could see plainly that not only was I not doing the things I enjoyed, I wasn't even doing the things I am good at. Most importantly, I asked myself the questions – over many weeks and months – What am I for? What is my purpose? I rediscovered the fact that my purpose is to bring ideas and beauty into the world. One of the ways I would do this would be to write. And if you have got this far, then the prophecy has in some way been fulfilled!

There are many ways to find the work we love. For me, decisions about what I will or will not do with the rest of my life are now so much clearer. My guiding principle is that the work should further my purpose, in a way that I enjoy. What a source of energy that is!"

On the other hand, Jo's approach has always been more straightforward and clear.

"Whenever I reach a fork in my life, I seem to choose the more exciting and interesting path. In this way, my major life decisions have been powered by great energy and relish for what life holds, instead of being occasions full of dread and worry. It doesn't mean that I have always made the right choices. Paths have taken me to dead ends, I've met obstacles on the way and I've sometimes missed some small yet fascinating side roads because I'm so convinced I know where I'm going . But it doesn't matter ... because I feel so very alive when I make my choices... and there are always more crossroads on the horizon!"

The American writer and motivational speaker Wayne Dyer summed this up with a very simple and powerful piece of advice. It's based on the idea that we all have something to contribute and that deep down, we already know our purpose, we've already heard, perhaps in dreams and reveries, the music we were meant to play. Dyer's advice is: *don't die with your music still in you.*

Chapter 9

Realign with your purpose –
what would you do if you knew you could not fail?

Maybe you now have a clearer or developing idea about your 'purpose'. How can you use that knowledge in practice? What kinds of things can you do to further your purpose? And what's stopping you from doing them right now?

The chances are that if you are still not convinced, what's holding you back is a fear of failure.

Suppose that you had always loved music and in your early years had wanted to be a musician. You play an instrument, but maybe not to a great professional standard. You love listening to music, going to concerts, reading about musicians. And when it gets right down to it, if you absolutely categorically *knew* you could not fail, you'd become a musician even now.

But there's the rub. You *don't* know that you could not fail, and given your inexpert level of musicianship, the likelihood of you failing would be very high.

You're stuck.

Or are you? One thing you could do is train yourself — or be trained — to be a better musician. But that's potentially time — consuming and expensive. Worth considering though, because not only is there a chance that it would pay off in the long run, but you would also most likely enjoy the process. Look again at what it is you like about music (or whatever that secret thing is, that you would do if you knew you could not fail). You don't just love playing — you love listening to music, going to concerts and reading about musicians. In no particular order, here are some options that you could consider.

☆ Open a music store specialising in the music you adore. In continental Europe there are shops specialising in world music and contemporary jazz, and what works in one place can often work in another. There could be an integral café that plays the music that you sell in the main part of the shop, and you could have a "Now Playing" sign that would encourage impulse buying of some piece of music that customers fall in love with, while they splash out on a cappuccino and croissant. It could be a cool place to hang out (and spend money!)

☆ Buy and sell musical instruments, either on the internet or in a traditional shop. You could become an expert in a particular type or range of instruments, and become the nucleus for a network of local musicians

☆ Write reviews of concerts for local papers, then for paper-based and internet magazines. You could interview musicians you admire, and sell the results to a publisher. Perhaps you find that you ask a particular question of all the musicians — something about the source of their creativity perhaps, and before you know it, you have an inspiring collection of articles that can be published as a book.

☆ Manage a musician or group of musicians. Find someone you really believe in. Make it your personal mission to see them get to the very top

☆ Become a concert promoter. Start small and work your way up to the Royal Albert Hall. Or defy conventional wisdom and do it the other way around!

The list is practically endless. So what would *you* do if you knew you could not fail?

Think about how you can immerse yourself in the area that you love, rather than tie yourself down to one particular way of earning a living. And bear in mind that you can build a *portfolio career*. All this means is that you don't have to put all of your eggs in one basket. You can find many different ways of earning a living, and all of them can be a source of enjoyment, fulfilment and success.

So ask yourself today — *what would I do if I knew I could not fail?* There are a hundred different ways of being successful, and deep down you already know what they are.

Chapter 10
Use your fear

There's a theory that there are really only two emotions — fear and love, and that you should always choose love.

But you'd have to be superhuman to control these two powerful emotions all of the time. Sometimes it just isn't possible to overcome fear, although we can do a lot to control it. Look at Chapter 21 — Control the state you're in — for some ways to be in command of your emotions, thoughts and even physiological states.

In fact, we know that there are only two 'natural' fears that we are born with — falling from heights and loud noises. The rest are learned as we go through life.

What has all this got to do with energy? Well, you can use your own fear to fuel your actions.

Let's take a very common example. Fear of public speaking is apparently the most common phobia. Ask someone who is genuinely cursed with this fear and they will leave you in no doubt as to the very real effect it has on their ability to function. Individuals use great ingenuity in inventing ways to avoid public speaking, and at almost any cost. And this doesn't have to involve a scenario where there are one hundred people in a room waiting to be informed and entertained: many are stricken simply by the thought of introducing themselves to three or four other people in the typical 'ice — breaker' scene, where each person is asked to give their name and some item of information about themselves.

Imagine if this fear could be turned into energy that would drive you out of your seat, powering your stride up to the front of the hall, fuelling your gestures, smiles and voice. Imagine that fear becoming the energy that makes your words ring out confidently, so the very source of your anxiety becomes the weapon used to defeat it.

Fear is internal energy produced to overcome an external or psychological threat.

What's the source of this fear? What is it? What can be done about it?

In the example of a fear of public speaking, the source is often traced back to early experiences in childhood, such as being ridiculed by parents or elder siblings when called on to speak. This external humiliation becomes a model: the young mind is very logical and sensitive and it quickly learns that it's dangerous to speak up. And the natural response to danger is fear.

Whatever the deep, perhaps hidden reason for whatever fears we may have, they are internalisations of something very real in the world. They should not be a source of shame. To some extent everyone carries fear in their soul at some time in life, and part of life's journey is to liberate oneself from fear forever. That's the long term goal.

So why is fear the response to danger? Perhaps it's simply the label we give to the subjective experience of the famous fight-or-flight reaction. When faced with danger, these are the two strategies that have served the long term evolution of our species: to run away or to fight. Both of these reactions cause complex changes in the body that prepare us for action. To return to the example of public speaking, there's often a negative feedback loop: physical changes make the breath more rapid and shallow, and the voice becomes weak and shaky. The shakiness increases our fear of humiliation, and suddenly we are in a vicious circle.

Enough of what fear is — *what can be done about it?*

Everyone has some form of fear and anxiety — it is the individual's ability to deal with fear that is important. Do you want to control it, or do you want to go on being terrorised and hobbled by fear?

The trick is to use the brain to change our thinking about the situation which causes us fear. If this sounds as though we are 'tricking' ourselves into not being fearful — that's right: that's exactly what we're doing. Here are some really effective ways to change fear into a different kind of positive energy:

- ✔ You are faced with a situation that makes you fearful. Imagine you are an actor. You are playing the part of a person who deals with great ease with this kind of situation. The character you are 'playing' is powerful, determined, good humoured and absolutely fearless. You play the part with gusto and skill. Imagine the scene at the end of your performance when you have come out of character and you're showered with bouquets and shouts of encore! If you want to, just stay in character!

- ✔ You are faced with a person, perhaps an authority figure, who makes you fearful. This time you are playing in a comedy–drama. Not only are you the fearless hero (really get into the part), but the fear-inspiring person has been inhaling helium and his or her voice is doing that Mickey Mouse thing. You, the fearless hero, are trying desperately not to laugh. Sometimes you don't quite succeed.

- ✔ Feel the fear. Examine it. It's little more than a set of physical reactions that are expressing themselves as energy in your body. Imagine that the fear is a gift, an energy that you can choose to use in any way you see fit. Now, use it to power your actions, your voice, your responses. Find the courage to expose yourself to situations where you're fearful, and get to know your feelings and reactions. Practice. Soon you'll see that your fear is also a set of unrealistic limitations which you have imposed upon yourself.

- ✔ Imagine the old fearful you. Be gentle with your old self: there's no need for condemnation or loathing. But now it's time to say goodbye to that way of living. You are now a more mature, balanced and fearless individual. What will you do with all that new energy at your disposal that used to be wasted on fear?

PART 3

❊

Energy Vampires and How to Deal With Them

If you hate a person, you hate something in him that is part of yourself. What isn't part of ourselves doesn't disturb us.

Hermann Hesse (1877—1962)

It seems that just about everyone knows an Energy Vampire and is trying hard to avoid them at all costs — which, by the way, is probably the best tactic. Funny though, no one ever seems to stand up and say — "Yes! An energy vampire! That's me you're describing!".

The energy vampires live at the centre of energy black holes. If you approach too closely you'll get sucked in — and just like a real cosmic black hole, time will stretch into infinity. Even light gets sucked into a black hole. Eventually though, you will arrive at the centre of the vampire's universe. And then what do you do?

This section has the tools to make sure you survive the encounter. Just like fear, we can use the experiences to make us stronger and even more energetic — it's all a matter of attitude and approach.

But first a word on Corporate Vampires. We hear many people complain that corporate life has something built into it that sucks the energy from us. Why is that? When will the owners and managers of organisations large and small recognise that the energy and creativity of their people is their greatest asset? Maybe you should give your manager a copy of this book!

But let's not lay the responsibility for our own energy, success and achievements at someone else's door. Bear in mind the thoughts of James Allen:

> *Man is made or unmade by himself. By the right choice he ascends. As a being of power, intelligence, and love, and the lord of his own thoughts, he holds the key to every situation.*

Chapter 11
Beat the vampire

Some people have the ability to walk into a room and have a massive negative effect on the energy available to us. The colour seems to drain from the world; there's an edginess and a feeling of dread, or simply resignation that this is going to be dull / tense / exhausting / all of the above.

Sometimes people who have this effect are authority figures. In the last chapter we discussed the fact that they have no power over us unless we choose to give it to them. We saw how to deal with this kind of energy sapper by using a spirit of playfulness and imagining ourselves as different kinds of characters. You can control your own internal states to protect your energy (also see Chapter 22 — *Do the Hardest Things First*).

There's another kind of energy sapper — the person who believes and acts as though the world is conspiring against them in everything that they do. All this person's effort is wasted, because they 'know' that any effort will end in defeat or humiliation. And if it isn't 'the world' that defeats them, it's the past, which was so hard, or the future, which will be even worse, or the boss, or the neighbours or the ex-spouse who ran off with someone else (and they wonder why?).

When you're around this kind of person for too long, you realise that they think a lot of their problems are *your* fault. Or you may find that you are being criticised about *your* attitudes to the world and *your* behaviour. This projection of the other person's problems onto you would be funny if it wasn't so painful for you!

The key to overcoming all of this is not to identify with the other person's state of mind. You can sympathise, you can try to help, but whatever you do, don't over-empathise. Don't let your body reflect the way they sit or walk or talk, or pretty soon your mind will be working like theirs too (except if you're trying our advanced technique — see below).

Don't feel guilty about not feeling the way that they do. That isn't your responsibility. In fact, if you really want to help the energy-sapper, keep your own energy high, be optimistic, be warm and funny and playful. Think of it as being like those safety instructions demonstrated on aircraft. If you have a child with you, make sure you put your own oxygen mask on first — if you don't safeguard yourself, you'll be in no position to help anyone else.

Most of us at some stage in our lives have felt undermined, undervalued and under attack. These feelings will sap your energy, demoralise you and can lead to you building a wall between yourself and your possibilities. Don't let that happen to you!

What are these feelings? What's real, out there in the world, and what is the product of your own mind?

Often we feel under attack from outside forces when the real problem is in our own attitudes and thinking. The first thing to realise is that no one has power over you, unless you give that power to them. Sure, someone may 'rank above' you in an organisation. They may be wealthier, or more successful, or be able to broadcast their opinions more effectively than you because of some power that they hold. But they cannot control your thoughts. Only you can do that.

Recognise honestly if you have given someone power over your reactions. Realise that only you could do this — you have chosen to give away your own control, or have just allowed it to happen by default.

So reach for your own oxygen mask first. The world is challenging, beautiful and inspiring. It's tragic that people who undermine you or sap your energy don't see it that way. But you don't have to compound the tragedy by seeing it their way. Help them to think and see and hear and touch and smell it in your way! See Chapter 22 for more on how you change not only your own state, but that of others too. And if that doesn't work, don't despair. In the end, you may just have to put distance between yourself and those who undermine you.

Technique!

Beating the Vampire is all about thinking and acting in your own way in the face of someone else's bad mood or unacceptable behaviour.

Technique 1: Basic Beat The Vampire

1. Notice the feeling in your body when someone first starts to drain your energy. Where is that feeling? Does it move?

2. Dissolve the feeling consciously. As you breathe in, imagine you are flooding that area of your body with light and energy.

3. If the feeling persists, reverse its motion. For instance, if you experience your reaction as a slowly spinning feeling in your abdomen, reverse the direction of the spinning and speed it up.

4. Keep an 'Energy Stance'. Stand tall, chin up, relaxed. Breathe steadily and deeply.

Technique 2: Advanced

1. Match the other person's body language. Stand or sit in the same way they do. Match their tone of voice, the speeds of their movement, and even their breathing rhythm. This creates a deep empathy.

2. Now start to change the way you talk, move and breathe. If speech was fast and manic, slow it down. If before you were sitting with head in hands, stand up and start to project your energy. Consciously bring the other person with you. Introduce lighter speech patterns, and talk about how good things are, not how bad.

3. At best you will have helped the other person. At worst, you will have remained in control of your own emotions and protected or increased your energy.

Chapter 12
Enjoyment is not a dirty word

Beneath the Indian Ocean, tectonic plates push in opposite directions, one against the other. Pressure and energy build, and something has to give. Eventually, one plate slides beneath the other, releasing vast amounts of energy as trillions of tons of rock are pushed a little closer to the centre of the earth. The planet wobbles on its axis for several hours, and the speed at which the earth rotates — and therefore the length of the day — is changed minutely, forever.

Close to the epicentre, buildings and lives are broken and flattened by the earthquake. A huge Tsunami builds, travels across the ocean, and takes many tens of thousands of lives over a vast area. The catastrophe is on a massive scale; people are left without houses, their boats, their livelihoods. Children are orphaned; parents lose whole families.

Across the world there is a massive outpouring of sympathy and practical help.

Meanwhile, run of the mill poverty, war, starvation and cruelty continue unabated, while the rich get richer. Our trading systems penalise the poor and worsen their situations. Our political systems deliver power to evangelising warmongers. The leaders of our religious systems prepare for more holy wars. The environment continues to degrade, the earth to groan under the weight of human 'progress'. Some scientists predict that the lethal combination of global dimming and global warming could cause unprecedented and irreversible destruction of life on earth in the next few decades.

Perhaps these environmental / political tragedies are even more deserving of our efforts than the victims of natural disasters, such as the 2004 Tsunami, which are brought about by geological facts of life. At least there may be something we can do about politics, religion, economics and the environment. We can use our energy to make the world a better place, if we so choose.

This is the same dilemma we face when it comes to dealing with energy-sapping individuals. We should not allow ourselves to get overwhelmed or paralysed. The sense of inadequacy in the face of natural disasters, the feeling of sadness and empathy with the victims, can give us the sense that we should not seek happiness for ourselves, that it's somehow flippant to do so. When tragic things happen closer to home — the painful illness or death of a loved one for instance — we feel this even more acutely.

Herbert Spencer once said:

> *No one can be perfectly free till all are free;*
> *no one can be perfectly moral till all are moral;*
> *no one can be perfectly happy till all are happy.*

What does this mean for someone who wants to maximise their energy? The first is to use our lives to free those who are not free. For some people this generates enormous power and they live life well.

A second reaction is to say that it's foolish to delay anything in life until perfection is achieved: take what you have now and make the most of it. Someone else once said:

> *Pain is inevitable; suffering is optional.*

That means it isn't circumstances that dictate the quality of life — it's our reactions to those circumstances.

It's ok to enjoy ourselves. It's more than ok. It is an important spiritual life principle. It's also a decision that you can take for yourself, and once that decision is taken, you'll find that there are huge stores of energy to power you through life.

Some people find life's meaning in suffering, which is seen as being noble. In Christian cultures the attitude runs deep, along with guilt, repression of instincts and the idea that the creation of beauty should be left to the hand of God. These are ideas that can shrink the soul, not expand it.

There's a world of enjoyment out there, and there should be no guilt attached to savouring it. Music, the arts, architecture; the beauty of thought itself, of meditation and contemplation; the beauty of human contact — physical, emotional and spiritual — these are the things that improve life, that drive us on to bigger and better things, that make it worth living.

Chapter 13
See the best in others

Seeing the best in others is one of the most powerful things you can do to boost your energy. And yet this somehow isn't obvious or intuitive. It may take a little explanation to bring you around to this approach!

Let's start with what this is *not*.

Seeing the best in others isn't about excusing the misdeeds of petty tyrants. It isn't about turning a blind eye to the bad behaviour of others so that you can have an easier life. Nor is it about indulging others in the hope that they grow out of anti-social behaviour that should be nipped in the bud immediately.

Seeing the best in others is mostly about you, and the act of raising your own awareness to the point at which you realise that you're not the centre of the universe. It's about understanding that the behaviour that we see isn't all about *us*, and that our readiness to take offence at some perceived insult is a function of our own minds and behaviour, not that of others. It's about being in control of our reactions, and not letting ourselves get caught up in bitterness and hatred.

The limited nature of human awareness makes it very difficult to see that not all communication out there is directed towards us. When we're insulted or hurt by what others say, it's often because we take general observations and comments about the world as specifically relating to us. This may or may not be the intended meaning of the communication.

There are a couple of principles to apply as you consider how to see the best in others. The first is that *the meaning of a communication is the response it gets*. When someone communicates to you with bitterness and cynicism, don't respond in kind. It may be that they are lost, blinkered and unable to look at themselves objectively. If you respond in kind, you not only change your own state to one of bitterness and cynicism, you also confirm to them that this is an appropriate state to be in. And so it goes on.

The second principle is that *people follow the best course of behaviour that they are currently capable of.* They are doing their best, given their view of the world at the present moment. However unreasonable or objectionable that behaviour may seem to you, there is absolutely no need to identify with it. Identification with the negative emotions or world-views of others will drain you of energy.

In the end, this business of seeing the best in others is all about the most energising thing in the world — your own freedom. If you condemn or judge those around you, it's your own freedom that's limited — not theirs. Judgement shrivels the heart and bludgeons the spirit. If you reap what you sow, and can expect to get back what you give, then are you sure that you will always be able to stand up to the judgement of others? Imagine yourself on the receiving end.

The other dimension to seeing the best in others is about giving praise, recognition and appreciation. Although some of us are lucky enough to be independent of the good opinion of others, this is not a common thing in human nature. Most people are silently crying out for recognition of their efforts, for appreciation of their intentions and actions. Touch someone with appreciation, and with no sense of expectation of anything in return, and marvellous things may happen. You will give people energy, and they will gladly give you energy back.

Chapter 14
To thine own self be true

> "*Mad, adj: Affected with a high degree of intellectual independence*"
> AMBROSE BIERCE (1842 - 1914), THE DEVIL'S DICTIONARY

There are few feelings as energising as this:

You speak your mind without fear. Your words unsettle those around you, but you carry on anyway — not for the sake of making people uncomfortable, but because the words need to be spoken. Your opinion and beliefs are out of place, but for that very reason, you must speak to show that your position isn't that of the majority; you know that to keep silent is to express agreement by default, and this you refuse to do. You make your point, without fear or favour.

In moments such as these we're truly alive. We're energised, alert and determined. There's an undercurrent of fear, but exhilaration wins out and sweeps us on in the right direction. If you've spoken from your own truth — and not merely because you want to be contrary, or are thinking about yourself and how you would like to stand out in the crowd — then you'll experience a moment that's bigger than your own ego-centred concerns. When values and our actions coincide we can sometimes stand amazed at the power this releases from within.

So why don't we do this more? Why have there been times in our lives when we should have spoken, but didn't?

Not speaking out when we know we should always comes down to the same thing — fear. Many of us were taught when we were young that children were to be seen and not heard. When we come into adult life, we sense that the power relations in work and other situations are just like those we saw in the family, and we are cast — or cast ourselves — in the role of child to someone else's adult (see the case study below).

Being a child can sometimes be very safe. We are protected by adults who also have the power to threaten and punish us, so it's a good thing to keep on the right side of them.

There is sometimes a fear that we could lose a job, or authority, or promotion etc, by speaking out. But is that kind of job worth keeping?

Sometimes outside of work there is a massive weight of conformity bearing down on us. The pressure is on to be just like everyone else, to keep quiet at awkward moments, to not declare that the Emperor has no clothes.

> *"If money is your hope for independence you will never have it. The only real security that a man will have in this world is a reserve of knowledge, experience, and ability"*
> HENRY FORD (1863 -1947)

But you are not a pack animal, are you?

What do you want energy for? So you can be more energetic in copying everyone else? So that you can hold your tongue and let the moment pass?

Case Study—

James and the Giant Adults

James worked in a company that made this adult–child relationship very explicit. Quite senior managers—though not at the very top of the organisation—insisted on calling the Board and the CEO 'the adults', which of course meant that James and his fellow workers were the children. So whatever was decided by 'the adults' had a distance from the employees; they could absolve themselves from moral responsibility for the direction the company went in. This language and symbolism was encouraged and used by 'the children', though that term was never used.

The company, which had a very long and proud tradition of independence, entrepreneurship and innovation (i.e. behaviour which suggested that everyone in the organisation had once regarded themselves as 'adult'), struggled in the market place.

What possible reason could there be for depicting the leaders of a company as 'the adults?' Perhaps it was no more than a harmless turn of phrase? James believed that the language implied several things:

– There was a 'command and control' structure. Most leading business thinkers see this as an increasingly inappropriate way to respond to modern business challenges, and the demands of rapidly changing marketplaces.

– Individuals were treated like children, and there were various child–like rituals. At its best this included displacement activities such as making fun of 'the adults' in team meetings. At its worst it was plain old bullying amongst the 'children'.

– Independent thinking was encouraged up to the point at which an idea failed. At that point, individuals were condemned and sometimes punished.

– The performance management system was designed in a way that gave people their objectives (the equivalent of 'tidy your room'?), rather than in a way that encouraged individuals to find unique, personal ways to contribute towards the company's aims.

> There are four things that anyone can do when a situation becomes intolerable:
> - change it
> - put up with it
> - walk away from it
> - change your response to it
>
> In this case, James decided to walk away. He reports that the company continues to struggle!

To be independent of the good opinion of others is liberating. It can also be lonely.

> *To thine own self be true, and it must follow, as the night the day, thou canst not then be false to any man.*
> SHAKESPEARE, HAMLET, ACT I, SCENE 3

But that loneliness will be short lived. You will get such a burst of energy from being your own man or woman that you'll be carried through the uncomfortable period where you might seem to an outcast, a social leper. Eventually, people will respect and admire you as an independent free thinker and a courageous person of principle. You don't have to be loud about it: you just have to know what your values are, and that you will not allow them to be compromised for the sake of a short-term tactical gain. So here are the things to remember when courage is failing, but you know you should speak out:

✔ The body will send you an early warning signal, even when your mind is suppressing the fact that you are being manipulated into a situation where you cannot be true to yourself. Listen and act on what your body already knows.

✔ It's better to be notorious and a little 'mad' than anonymous and herded like a sheep.

✔ In the long run you'll be remembered as a person of principle, and that's worth more than short-term popularity.
✔ The best people encourage independence and individuality. Shun those who don't. You will still be successful — probably more successful in the long run.
✔ You are a unique and worthwhile individual. Live your own truth.

Chapter 15
Your enemy was sent to help you

Imagine for a moment that your whole life is a test. The test doesn't involve counting how much money or property you end up with. Nor does it measure fame or power over others.

The purpose of the test is to measure how much peace of mind you're able to experience. This includes happiness, contentment, excitement, ecstasy, calmness and freedom from worry, jealousy and hatred.

For some people, the idea that this could possibly be the purpose of life will seem selfish and shallow. Surely we were meant to suffer? Surely we were meant to feel the pain of others, and help alleviate that pain?

No — in our humble opinion, you weren't meant to suffer in this life, you were meant to learn and have fun, to discover some truths about yourself and others, and move through life with compassion, commitment and energy.

So imagine this: when there is someone in your life who seems to have been sent expressly to make you feel angry, frustrated and sad — realise that *your enemy was sent to help you!*

Now this is a subject that a friend of ours called Louise has had plenty of experience of. And what took her months and years to learn, you might just be able to pick up in the next couple of hundred words…

Case Study—

Harry and Louise

Harry was uncouth to say the least. He swore, told bad and filthy jokes at inappropriate moments, acted as though Louise supported his humour and approach, and was all in all the coarsest, loudest and most stupid man she ever met.

Sometimes it was really hard to just be in the same room with Harry. He was a work colleague and hard for Louise to get away from. When it finally occurred to her that this man was actually a blessing, that he had been sent to try her as part of the game of life, everything changed. The louder and coarser Harry became, the funnier it seemed. It became obvious that his behaviour wasn't personally directed at Louise–for whatever reason, this was just his role in the game. It dawned on Louise that she wasn't at the centre of the universe–in the grand scheme of things, her being offended was just laughable.

Over time Louise came to realise that what lay at the root of her problem was that she was an expert at being offended. Not only offended at the behaviour of others in close relationships, but at the habits or even presence of total strangers in the briefest of encounters. In fact, as Louise got more skilful at being offended (many of us are taught to do this as young children) she found that she could regard practically anything as a personal affront. Her house was too cold or too warm, there was too much traffic sent specifically to delay her, the rain was sent to inconvenience her, the sole purpose of the sun was to blind her when driving. She was one offended person!

> Then Louise read something that helped to change her whole outlook. The unlikely source was the books of Carlos Castenada. Castenada describes his adventures in the outlandish world of a Mexican sorcerer, where he's taught that one of the greatest gifts in life is to be sent an enemy. An enemy is a blessing. An enemy is sent by unknown powers to give us shortcuts to knowledge and happiness, to expose our egos as childish and shallow, and to let us laugh at our own fears and shortcomings.

Like a lot of the advice in this book, acting as if your enemy was sent to help you relies upon you making a choice. You can play this curious game and pretend, for the sake of experiment, that the person in your life right now who is making things difficult for you is your greatest ally in disguise, and that every thing they do is designed to help you. Or you can continue to be angry, frustrated and offended. ***You can increase your energy, or you can have your hurt ego burn it up and squander it.***

When Louise chose to see Harry as an ally, there was an immediate change. Her spirit was lighter, resilience a hundred times greater, and she was able to free up the huge amounts of energy she'd put into being offended. Over time though, something else happened. As Louise played this game of imagining that Harry was her ally, she noticed things about him that she'd never seen before. Harry had his own problems, and at Harry's core there was something tender and vulnerable. His behaviour was really nothing more than the defensive strategy of an insecure man. In short, it turned out that Harry was just like the rest of us. The point is, it wasn't Harry who had changed, it was Louise. Before, she had needlessly generated all the fear, anxiety and frustration that made every moment in that workplace seem like hell.

Since then, Louise's energy levels are increased a hundredfold, and she rarely gets frustrated at the behaviour of others.

When you find yourself in this situation, play the game and see that "difficult person" as your ally.

PART 4

❄

Respond or React

Ultimately, the only power to which man should aspire is that which he exercises over himself.

Elie Wiesel

This part of the book is all about choice. It's easy to forget that we have a choice about how we respond to external circumstances. In most situations in life, it's our conditioned reactions to what we encounter, rather than the actual events, which make us de-energised, frustrated or hurt. But we can choose to build positive representations about the world around us and indeed about our own feelings, thoughts, and ideas.

Use your energy and freedom to decide how you respond to the world around you.

This section will give you some incredibly powerful tools and ideas to help you do just that. In fact, it's not just about how you 'respond' — it's also about setting yourself up to become energised and effective in everything you do. That includes moving towards what you want in life, and away from what you don't want. It includes 'tricking' your brain into believing that you can dominate your circumstances — because your reality will change once you turbo-charge it with belief.

Then you can make choices that energise you and fulfil your hopes and dreams.

Chapter 16
Live your dream today

Every day, you reinvent yourself. You do this unconsciously through a process of reinterpreting the past, and your emotional responses to it. Your emotional responses in turn have been conditioned by how you have learned to think. Often, we believe that our upbringing told us only how to act, but we also have habitual patterns of feeling and thinking that we slip into in response to what's happening around us.

So there are two aspects to the way that we continually make our own reality. The first is to do with how we think, and the second has to do with the way we recycle the past.

The patterns of thought and feeling we use can be the most energy-draining and destructive forces in our lives. In later sections you'll see exactly how to change those patterns so that you support — rather than undermine — yourself. This section concentrates on the other area where we can make massive positive changes — the way we recycle the past.

A person with massive positive energy doesn't solve this problem with a new and effective way of reinterpreting the past. *Our aim is to reinterpret the future.* Leave the past alone if you feel it undermines you — what's done is done, and everything that has happened has led you perfectly to this point in your life where you are studying ways to bring new positive energy into your reality. There's no need for shame or guilt about the past. You're ready to dream a future where you'll use the talents and skills you have to create a wonderful life.

There are many things you can do to bring your dreams closer to reality, but today and for the rest of this week let's try to re-condition your brain so that it naturally steers you towards the future you want to create. You do this when you *live the dream today.*

First take an aspect of what you want your life to be like. It could be connected with your relationships with others, to your spiritual needs and desires, or your dreams of wealth, success or achievement.

There's a simple exercise that teaches your brain to understand how glorious that future will be. Once you can do this regularly, you'll find yourself automatically behaving in a way that will bring about the future you want. You will find yourself drawn to the people, places and situations that support your plan of action, and you'll be inspired and encouraged by your own thinking. Your internal dialogue — the 'voice' that offers a running commentary on your every action and thought — will stop being the discouraging whiner that you put up with in the past, and will be a source of energy and encouragement.

Before you try the next exercise, read through once first, then go back and do each step. Better still, get a friend to read it aloud for you, as you close your eyes and go deeply into your imagination.

Technique!

Future You

1 Sit comfortably where you won't be disturbed. Breathe easily, and quieten the mind. Be aware of your breath as it passes through your nostrils.

2 With your eyes closed, think of yourself in the future, as though you had already achieved your dream. See yourself as you will be then. Look closely at yourself—your facial expression, how you greet and react to other people, how you hold your body, how you exude a quiet but powerful confidence. Is the picture black and white? What happens if you picture yourself in full, glorious colour? What happens if

you turn up the brightness, saturate the colours, and magnify the picture? Experiment. Get the picture just right. Watch how you move through your day.

3 Now listen to the sounds around this new, future you. Are they harsh or soft, quiet or loud? Is there music, happy voices, silence? What about the pitch of the sounds you hear? Get it just right, hear the sounds as they will be in your successful future. What are people saying?

4 What do you feel? Is there a warm spring breeze on your skin? Are your clothes soft and comfortable, and do people greet you with a welcoming touch? Imagine what the future feels like.

5 What about aromas and taste? Are you eating healthy, tasty food that leaves you feeling light and energised? What does the future taste and smell like? Is there perhaps a jasmine scent on the breeze? Or do you have the salt smell of the ocean or clear mountain air lifting your spirits?

6 Bring all of the elements together. Let your brain take it all in, realising how life will be when you have moved into the future of your dreams.

7 Stop the movie of yourself at your favourite point. Take that still picture and put a border around it. Make the border your favourite, inspiring colour.

8 Imagine the photograph in a magazine. What caption would it have? Give it a caption now.

That's all there is to it. If it felt easy and pleasant, as though you didn't have to put too much effort into the process—great! That's how it's meant to be. You are programming your brain to expect the best for you, and move you towards the future you imagine for yourself. Now carry that vision of yourself into the rest of your day, and act as if you have already achieved what you're setting out to do. Don't worry that this will make you complacent—it won't. You are simply bolstering your confidence, marshalling your skills and resources to see how wonderful your future could be. Live your dream today and you will see, hear and feel that you are creating your future moment by moment, and it starts right now!

Chapter 17
Stop! Look at the bigger picture!

> *There is only one wisdom: to recognise the intelligence that steers all things.*
> HERACLITUS

Despite several 'religious revivals', Western society is still overwhelmingly secular. Church attendances continue to fall, and despite the increased fundamentalism there's still a feeling that the established churches fail to cater for those people with a need to find deeper meaning in their lives. Whether members of established churches or not, many are struggling to find meaning in a civilisation that seems to be intent on violence and exploitation.

So where's the 'energy angle' in all this?

Look at your own difficulties and compare them to the problems all around you. Perhaps your own concerns will start to look smaller.

There are really only two things you can do — resign yourself to the way of the world, or make a conscious effort to change it. When you choose the latter, your energy is massively increased. Ironically, the weight of the world is no longer on your shoulders — you're too conscious of the weight being on the shoulders of others. There's another angle to this idea of changing the world though. A friend recently told us this story about an old man, looking back on his life... the man says:

When I was a young man, I wanted to change the world. I found it was difficult to change the world, so I tried to change my nation. When I found I couldn't change the nation, I began to focus on my town. I couldn't change the town and as an older man, I tried to change my family. Now, as an old man, I realize the only thing I can change is myself, and suddenly I realize that if long ago I had changed myself, I could have made an impact on my family. My family and I could have made an impact on our town. Their impact could have changed the nation and I could indeed have changed the world.

The great men and women of history had massive energy because they devoted themselves to something larger than their own egos and circumstances. Whether we look at the works of great artists, philosophers, or scientists, we see them striving for truth and beauty that is at the heart of what it really means to be human. But we believe that they started their work on themselves.

Ancient traditions, particularly those of the east such as Taoism, suggest that there's a universal energy flowing through everything, and that this energy is the very stuff of life. Physicists, mathematicians and Life Scientists are studying systems at almost unimaginable levels of detail and finding that the further we look, the less we find. There is an organising principle, but somehow it will not reveal itself to electron microscopes. In the end there is only energy.

The universe is energy that can be accessed by everyone in a way that allows us to draw what we need into our lives. If it's true that we come from the same source of energy that created everything else in the Universe, then our main task in life is to get aligned with that energy and use it to find answers.

Perhaps the simple answer is that 'good' energy is simply health and happiness, and that's really the big picture.

So, once again, I ask you to suspend your disbelief. Imagine if you will that there is an organising principle in the Universe that causes energy to manifest in an infinite variety of ways. You are one of those varieties. You are here to play out some time as a 'human being'. What were you before? And what will you be when you are no longer human?

How will you play while you are here?

Enjoy the game.

Chapter **18**

Take responsibility

One of the most energising things that you can do that will have an immediate effect is to take responsibility — even for things which you know should be taken care of by someone else.

Taking responsibility for things can work on several levels, and all of them will give you a massive energy boost. The most important way of using the power of responsibility though, is to *take ownership of the results you produce*. Recognise that, wherever you are right now, you are solely responsible for getting yourself to this point. You and only you.

Perhaps you're thinking that just isn't fair. Maybe you've had setbacks and circumstances in your life that have held you back, or people who messed up and left you to face the consequences. You have dependents to look after, you're trapped by your mortgage — and on and on it goes.

But if it's true that you're not responsible in every way for the results you have already obtained, and you believe that it's never possible to be wholly responsible, then you are admitting that you are not in control of your own life. What's the point of planning for the future if you have no control, if you give away your right and ability to own the outcomes of your own plans and actions?

Do yourself a favour and get a massive energy boost right now by rejecting that way of looking at things. *Take responsibility now*. What do you want to become? What is your greatest ambition? What would you do if you knew that you were solely responsible for the outcome?

Well, you *are* solely responsible for the outcome. It's all your responsibility. Who else's could it be?

This new way of looking at ownership of results works on a day to day basis. Think about those times at work when you or other people have dragged their feet, hoping that someone else will step into the breach. There's a loss of energy, awkward silence, and a general sheepishness. You can be the one who breaks through all that, takes the bull by the horns, and gets on and does whatever needs doing. Two things will happen—you'll feel better about yourself, even if those around you are muttering or rejoicing that you have saddled yourself with something that was better avoided. Secondly, if you persistently step forward and take responsibility for what needs to be done, you'll get a reputation that will spread like wild fire.

A few years ago Peter worked for a San Francisco-based company that was expanding into Europe with London as its base for operations. The company was growing more quickly than its admin procedures—and its people—could cope with, and as the manager responsible for the London operation, Peter quickly realised that there were some urgent "issues". For example, London needed to hire high calibre people in substantial numbers with next to no support from the San Francisco based HR department; the building where the operation was based was unfinished, and the work needed to get done quickly and to a high standard; there was no tea or coffee for the staff; there were no fire extinguishers or fire licence granted by the inspection authorities; there were no office supplies; there was no photocopier or fax machine.; there was no process for dealing with customer complaints, or to make sure that everything done in London supported the company's global policy.

At that point, it would have been easy to sit back and whine about the lack of organisation and support from facilities, HR and all the rest back in sunny California. But those folks were doing their best too—they weren't deliberately making life hard for others, and if they could have waved a magic wand to make it all better, they would have.

This is what Peter did.

"I hired good people as quickly as I could. I reasoned that it was more

dangerous for the company to wait until HR got its act together, than it was for me to ignore some of the bureaucratic niceties. And I took full responsibility for that decision. I supervised and took responsibility for the remaining building work, and could often be found with screwdriver in hand, finishing a detail somewhere in the offices. I invited the fire inspectors into the office spaces, got their advice on what I needed to do, and did it with no approval from Head Office. With little or no hope for a return on my money, I went out and bought tea, coffee and all the paraphernalia to go with it, and visited a local Office Equipment store with my own credit card. Once the photocopier and fax had arrived, and seeing that no one had made provision for their installation, I moved them and connected them myself.

If all this sounds crazy — and I bet you are thinking of at least a few reasons why some of the things I did were not a good idea — at the time it seemed the thing to do, because no one else was going to do it for me.

The results? Well, I had great staff in place in record time, the London Office was launched on time and in spectacular style, my staff were safer and happier (and less thirsty!). I was rapidly promoted several times and was soon responsible for the global operation, which meant working with some wonderful people in beautiful far flung places across the globe. The experience of taking responsibility for all of those things (which by the way, I learned as I went along) was invaluable. Oh, and I more than doubled my salary within a year."

Remember, whatever the circumstances — you are in charge. Choose how to respond to your circumstances, ignore conventional wisdom if necessary, and do what needs to be done.

Chapter **19**

Be in control

It may be that you've come to this section of the book because for some reason, things are getting you down. Perhaps you feel that there's a loss of control in your life, that others are calling the shots, that you have no choices, or only bad ones. Let's turn that around over the next few pages.

Dominating your circumstances is about being in control of your responses to what's happening around you. If you identify with your emotions, you can get caught in a downward spiral of negative responses to difficult situations. We become the thing we hold in our minds; we invest so heavily in the situations around us that we can't see where the circumstances end, and we begin.

So the first thing to realise is that *you are not your circumstances.* You have an integral worth, quality and existence entirely separate from what is all around you, and no power on earth can alter that fact.

As an illustration, let's take an extreme situation where we seem to be dominated by the conditions we're in, where there's a minimum of choice, and the exercise of free will seems impossible. An example of this would be if you were in prison.

In prison—so we're told!—you have little or no control over when and what you eat, who you live, work and play with or how you spend your leisure, work, or any other time. You cannot easily choose when to sleep or wake if you're close to noisy people with other ideas, and you have next to no control over whom you associate or do not associate with. The list could go on and on. Almost every aspect of life is impacted. There seems to be a total lack of freedom.

But there is one aspect of life which no one can deprive you of— your ability to think. No one can really get inside your head and control your thought patterns if you don't grant them permission. You may be forced into behaving in a certain way given the extreme circumstances you are in — but *you are not your behaviour*.

What you are to a large extent is your thoughts, and the choice you have about the way you think. Thoughts in turn allow you to control your emotional responses to even the worst of circumstances.

As we mentioned, sometimes it's all too easy to identify with our emotions. In fact, the real problem is that we allow the wrong emotions to gain control of us, and we do that because we give up control of our own thought processes. We react to our lack of freedom in a way that gives the feeling of powerlessness a huge boost of energy. We give those who imprison us increased power by validating them through our own thoughts. So what's the answer?

What's needed is a burst of energy for our own feelings of control, our own thoughts, and our own ability to creatively think and feel our way into a newer, better set of circumstances. A reaction is instinctive and uncontrolled. A response is measured and effective. The aim is to respond, and not to react.

When you say to yourself — I am in control — you are speaking the truth. In the end, you control yourself. Think the thought, give it power, then amplify that power. Feel yourself as an intelligent, independent person with all the resources you need to change the situation, and be absolutely certain that these thoughts cannot be taken away from you. They stand.

There are some very practical ways of being in control.

Think for a moment about how you feel in a situation where you need to impose yourself, your beliefs, and your values, but somehow are unable to do it. In these situations people feel inadequate, weak, unconfident, unsure that their contribution is of value, or some combination of all these things. With practice you can get yourself out of this disempowered state in a few moments. You can choose to be in any state you wish.

Before you try the next exercise, read through once first, then go back and do each step. Better still, get a friend to read it aloud for you, as you close your eyes and go deeply into your imagination.

Technique!
Being In Control

Find a calm, quiet and comfortable place to practice the technique. Later on, you'll be so good at this that you'll be able to do it on the fly, anytime, anywhere.

Take a few quiet breaths and clear your mind. Think of a time when you felt powerful. Remember a situation when you were massively competent, strong, confident, and sure that what you had to offer was valuable. If you really can't think of an episode like that from your own past, imagine what it would be like if you were in that powerful state.

Look closely at the memory or imagined situation. What does it look like? Would you be more empowered and motivated if the image you see was brighter? Try that now. How about more colour? And try making the image bigger, or smaller, or whatever makes it even more empowering for you.

Pay attention to the sounds, feelings and even smells in your memory or imagination of this empowered you. Try changing those factors–warmer, more mellow sounds, louder–whatever it is that does it for you, that makes you feel as confidently in control as it's possible to be. Are you in the picture you have created, or do you see it as if through your own eyes? Try both ways to see which is the most powerful for you.

The trick now is to make those thoughts and feelings of power and confidence accessible to you at all times. We can do this very easily by creating an 'anchor'. When you reach the point just before your feelings of confidence are highest, give yourself a signal that you can later associate with those feelings.

My own 'anchor' for self–confidence and motivation is a very simple gesture–I press my thumb and first finger together at the point at which I feel fired up and confident. Repeat this process a few times–when you are imagining yourself at–or just before–the peak of the state that you want to be in, 'anchor' that state with a gesture or a word. Then when you need to be in that resourceful state, all you need to do is make that gesture–which can be very inconspicuous to others–to put yourself in a wonderful, energised, powerful frame of mind and activity. The effect is instantaneous.

Be in control!

Chapter 20
A week full of gumption

> *Thousands of people have talent. I might as well congratulate you for having eyes in your head. The one and only thing that counts is: Do you have staying power?*
> NOEL COWARD

Having gumption is about persisting when the going gets tough — whether you are training to be a fighter pilot, or are breast feeding your baby!

One of the delights of writing this book has been the way in which it's been relevant to what is going on in the real world. Sometimes, as difficulties have arisen we've looked back at our own thoughts and techniques, and used them to kick-start the day. Funny then that over the last few days, there have been excuses in abundance to do anything but the difficult (though pleasant) duty of writing this book, something which, as Noel Coward would agree, we know we have the talent for. But talent is nothing. What we need is gumption!

Gumption.

That feels better already. The word itself is an energy boost. Gumption is the quality on which all achievement is built — civilisations, cities, empires, works of art, even simply feeding ourselves and our families. It's a common quality, but not so common and easy to use that we can take it for granted.

People who have massive energy, and make important contributions to life have gumption. It's the quality that above all else marks out successful people.

What exactly is gumption? Dictionaries tell us that it's a Scottish word meaning:

~ *drive and initiative*
~ *shrewd or spirited initiative and resourcefulness*
~ *enterprising spirit*
~ *go (!)*
~ *ready practical sense*

In fact, gumption is just about the only thing you'll ever need — especially if things aren't going entirely to plan. When people have stopped believing in you or your ideas, or the Universe itself seems to be refusing to act in a manner which supports your objectives — that's when you need gumption.

Gumption is what will keep driving you on, because gumption *is* self-belief. It's a practical and inspired belief in your ability to get to where you are going, and it's a stubborn refusal to give up when all about you have lost faith. Gumption is therefore strength of character, willpower and even vision. Gumption will tell you that your dream is possible, that the fact that others can't see what you see is their problem and not yours, and that you will succeed if you have faith in yourself.

There are many stories about inventors whose experiments 'fail' over and over again, until at last, one day, the experiment 'works'. Gumption is what kept them going, because they knew that *there's no such thing as failure — there are only results*. If the things that you are doing are not getting you what you want — *do something else*. Gumption is the strength, willpower and discrimination of your intellect when it realises that it must change its strategy in order to get the results it desires.

So how do we generate gumption? Can it be generated, or are we given a finite supply at birth?

Gumption can be generated. But it's not the same thing as stubbornness. Stubbornness is only appropriate once you have used your brain to examine your strategies and behaviours, and are sure that you're on the right track. A refusal to change an opinion about the shape of the earth, because our visual sense tells us it's flat, isn't an example of gumption. It's an example of sticking with inappropriate beliefs in the face of new evidence.

So the first way to generate gumption is to stop reacting to the outside world and the information it provides us with. Gumption can only be generated and used once we have weighed the options, possibilities, and the impossibilities. So gumption is generated by taking the time to think before we act. Then we can act with confidence, strength and unbending will.

The second way to generate gumption is to *practice flexibility*, also known as using our 'sensory acuity'. Be sensitive to what the world is telling you about the results you get, and be flexible enough to change when you realise that your strategy can be refined for better results.

Having gumption means being strong and intelligent enough to continually make minor adjustments to the direction you're going in, like a helmsman at the rudder. Gumption is not the part of us that says 'I've set my course and I know I set it right, so nothing will convince me to review my decisions, even if I seem to be temporarily off course'. No, that part of us has a completely different name!

Interestingly, the kind of behaviour that says 'I will not change' is often seen in business where 'change' is a fashionable concept, and what every progressive manager and leader is meant to sign up to. In fact, the most common place you see inflexibility and a refusal to use sensory acuity to alter direction is in *change* projects themselves! These projects start off with objectives that are often outmoded and irrelevant before they are half finished, but nobody dare say so. So the one common quality of failed change projects is a stubborn refusal to change!

But back to you, and how to generate gumption. One final way we will mention is to use the technique of remembering a time when you were successfully full of gumption in the past, and getting yourself into that same resourceful state so that you can be full of gumption again, right now. But that happens to be the subject of the very next chapter!

Chapter 21
Control the state you're in

We've touched on this subject a few times, and now we'd like to delve into it more deeply. This section is all about how you can quickly and easily move from one state of mind (and body and soul) to another. Imagine the power of being able to change your state at will—from one where you lack motivation, are depressed and devoid of energy, to one where you are full of life, power, determination and happiness.

An important finding of modern holistic approaches to health—including Neuro-Linguistic Programming (NLP), which is where we can find some really useful techniques for changing the state we're in—is that the mind and body are intimately connected, and in a way which many people don't guess at.

To illustrate this, think about how a depressed person looks. There's a certain 'depressed' way of holding the body. Shoulders are hunched, head bowed, facial expressions sad, voice muted. Even the hands express sadness, and breathing is often slow and shallow, or can be heard as a deep sigh.

Intuition tells us that the mind has caused our bodies to display these visible signs of depression. One of the remarkable insights of NLP has been to show that the relationship between mind and body often works in the opposite direction—in other words, changing your body can automatically bring about a change in the quality of your mood, thoughts and feelings.

Change your physical stance and body processes, and your mind will follow! Try it right now.

Read through once first, then go back and do each step.

> ## Technique!
>
> ### Use Your Body to Change Your Mood
>
> Stand up from your chair. Step into a confident position.
>
> Straighten your spine gently so that your shoulders are slightly back, but relax your body as much as you can. Bend the knees slightly, just so they are aren't locked.
>
> Take a deep breath in through your nose. Feel energy coming into your body with every breath, and be aware that this energy is your connection with the Universe.
>
> As you take in the next deep breath through your nose, and down into your belly area, raise your arms in a gesture of joyful welcome as though you are meeting a long lost loved-one at an airport.
>
> Let your head go back, as though your energy is coming from the sky itself. As the energy flows through you, allow yourself to smile.

Now, I defy you to tell me that you were able to feel sad or depressed through that sequence! You changed your physiology and your mind followed. It's that simple.

There's more though.

The technique above put you into a receptive, relaxed, energetic state of being that can form the basis for whatever even more resourceful state you want to access. So that's next. We've looked at this before, but it's worth going over again.

There are three parts to the process of "changing state".

First, remember in detail what it was like to be in such a state in the past (or imagine what it would be like to be in one).

Second, amplify the qualities of those feelings, sounds, pictures, etc that you associate with being in a resourceful state.

Finally, 'anchor' the resourceful state with a simple gesture that you can use later to immediately invoke the state that you want.

Before you try the next exercise, read through once first, then go back and do each step. Better still, get a friend to read it aloud for you, as you close your eyes and go deeply into your imagination.

Technique!
Change Your State

#1 Access a past state
Sit in a comfortable chair with your feet flat on the floor and your hands and shoulders relaxed. Close your eyes. Let your thoughts quieten. Breathe in gently through the nose. Think of some time in the past when you were in the state that you now wish to be in. Let's say that state is one of supreme self-confidence (you can do this for any state—success, energy, achievement, concentration, determination, etc). If you can't remember being in that state, imagine what it would be like if you were.

#2 Amplify the feelings you experienced in that past state
Notice everything about the scene now playing in your mind. Are you in the picture you're remembering (can you see yourself?). Or do you see the scene as if through your own eyes? Try to switch from one to the other. If you find that changing your perspective makes the feelings of confidence stronger for you, then stay with that. Now notice the quality of the image. Is it in black and white, or colour? Is it sharp, fuzzy, large and close, small and distant? Where is the image in relation to you?.

Slightly up and to the left? Or directly in front? Now play with all of these visual qualities of your memory. Try making the image brighter, larger, more colourful. Experiment until it most strongly evokes the most wonderful feelings of confidence.

Now do the same thing for the other elements of your memory—sounds, smells, tactile sensations. What do you hear, touch and smell? Try making sounds softer or louder, clearer or more 'woolly'; make feelings smoother, or warmer, or cooler. Intensify your memory of the honeysuckle that happened to be on the breeze. Feel the wellbeing increasing as you fine tune your memory or imagined scene.

#3 Anchor this new state you are in
Just at (or just before) the point when your feelings of confidence (or success, or happiness, etc) are at their most powerful, 'anchor' the state you're in by associating it with a gesture or a word that you can use later to recall the state that you want to be in. For example, just as you are at the peak of happiness, tap the outside of your knee. Then go back to the start of the process, and repeat it once or twice, so that you again associate the tap on the outside of your knee with the resourceful state that you want to invoke. Leave the process for a few minutes, then tap the outside of the knee again. This will automatically generate the state of confidence that you want to be in.

Keep practising!

Another interesting technique uses your imagination about the future. The power of this is in the way you use your body as well as your mind. Remember, don't just read these exercises — they really do work but you have to give them your best shot!

Technique!
Step Into the Future

1. Stand in a large room that has plenty of space, or somewhere outside like a garden where you can move freely.

2. Stand relaxed and imagine a scene that is roughly one week in the future.

3. Where do you see the image of that scene? Most people will see it in front of you and possibly slightly to your left. Where is it for you? Notice how far away from you it is.

4. Now do the same for other times in the future. Imagine an event one month, six months and a year into the future. See where these events appear in relation to where you're standing. They probably extend off in front of you, or to the side.

5. Now, imagine a fantastic future, where all your dreams are coming true. Imagine what will happen in one week, one month, six months and one year from now to create the perfect world for you.

6. Step into the first position, where you saw yourself in one week's time, in your wonderful future. Feel what it's like to be in that future. Hear what you'll hear, taste what you'll taste and feel what you feel. Then step into the one month position and do the same thing. Then repeat for six months and a year. Make sure you physically step into each position.

What you've just done is to programme your mind and body for success!

Chapter 22
Do the hardest things first

A sure-fire recipe for depression, low energy, frustration and lack of achievement is to put off doing the thing that is the hardest. Over the years, people become experts at this. But you can wean yourself off the habit by adopting a better strategy. That's what we're going to describe now.

Very often, we put off doing what we need to do without even thinking about it. The decision-making process seems to be missing entirely, but at some hidden level below the conscious thought processes, we know there's some unpleasant task or duty lurking. Sometimes the task even makes our to-do list, but just as often, it doesn't even get a mention. And yet we obsess about it all day, allowing it to drain us of energy, and to cast its shadow over everything we do. The shadow is cast by guilt and a kind of lack of self-respect, because we beat ourselves up for not doing what we feel should be done.

Let's say that the task in question is that you feel obliged to call your friend who you 'know' is going to bring you down with his negative attitude to everything under the sun. The worst part about not doing the task *isn't that it doesn't get done* — it's the effect it has on everything else that you have planned for the day. It has a negative effect on your thoughts, your feelings, your actions and your energy. It's the saboteur of your true intentions. Once you really know that fact, you will feel much more motivated to not let it happen — to save your day from sabotage.

Another thing to realise that it isn't always as bad as we imagine it will be. You eventually make the call and find that your depressing friend has both won the lottery and fallen in love. He's delighted to hear from you and full of encouragement for your schemes and dreams which he usually belittles and derides. Okay, unlikely, but it happens sometimes!

So why do we put off doing things? Because we're attracted to the prospect of pleasure and repelled by the promise of pain. We steer clear of unpleasant things. If our friend always depresses us, then we will quite naturally want to avoid him, even if we know he needs help (and just in passing, we notice that our friend's behaviour describes a vicious circle that guarantees that he'll drive away more people, become more lonely, and have yet more to whinge about).

So we think we know what the effects of calling our friend will be. We'll be frustrated, depressed and probably angry by the time we've finished talking to him. And don't you just know that the first thing he'll complain about is the fact that you haven't called in a month, thus neatly placing some of the blame for his situation on you. But what we don't take into account is the effect of the slow torture of not calling him, which seems to get worse every day.

The fact is that a decision needs to be made. Either don't call—in which case don't *ever* call—or call right now.

We'll come back to this in a moment. But let's imagine for the moment that you make the call.

So what would be the benefits of changing this behaviour in general, and of making that particular call that we've been discussing? Well, a massive weight will immediately be lifted from your shoulders. You'll be energised for the rest of the day and this will happen whether or not your friend brings you down with his whinging, because it isn't his whinging that is really at issue—it's your ability to face it. If you face the situation, make a decision and act on it, it almost doesn't matter about the details of the outcome. The fact is that you will have gained in strength, in power, and in self-respect.

Then how do you do it? How do you screw up your courage and take action?

First of all, examine what is really happening here. What's the underlying dynamic of the situation? If you dread writing reports, or operating some noisy piece of machinery, or driving on the motorway, and that's the thing that you are putting off, and yet it's an integral part of your job, then I have a newsflash for you.

You need to change your job!

Look at the real underlying situation, and work out a strategy that means that you never again have to suffer the dread of putting things off. In the example we've been discussing, is the friend who habitually puts you down, belittles your efforts, and depresses you with his problems really a friend? We all need help now and again, but the person who has the knack of making you depressed knows at some level that they have that power, and they choose to use it. In the same way, you can choose your friends. Or you can have a one-time-only discussion with them that plainly states that you aren't prepared to be a doormat any longer, and that if the friendship is to survive, you both need to share good things as well as bad. If that doesn't work—find yourself some new friends.

Here's another tactic—*outsource!* Maybe what you are putting off is something that absolutely needs to be done—but you just hate to do it. Perhaps you run a small business and have to keep your books and file tax returns. It is your idea of hell. Well, pay someone else to do it. Find a way. If you think that it's not cost effective to do that, remember that it isn't just the time it would take you to do the task that you can offset against the expense of having someone else do it for you—it's the cost of the time you spend doing worthless things just in order to avoid doing what you really need to do! It's the cost of your lost energy, and your lost opportunities.

Another way to face the hardest task you have is to break it down into more manageable chunks, each of which is bearable on its own. This is one you have to be really careful with. It's very easy to break down an unpleasant task into ten different things—nine of which are easy. So you do the easy one first, and the tenth never gets done. All you have done is devised a new strategy for wasting your time and avoiding the real issue.

Face your fears and do what you dread to do, but know has to be done. You will feel energised, liberated and powerful.

This is the power of doing the most difficult thing first!

PART 5

✻

Energy Angels!

There is overwhelming evidence that the higher the level of self–esteem, the more likely one will be to treat others with respect, kindness, and generosity.

Nathaniel Branden

Some people just seem to energise those around them, and attack everything they do with verve and passion. Their language is always upbeat, and they put a positive spin on even the most difficult of circumstances. These are good people to attract into your life, because they're the ones who will support and encourage you, rather than undermine your efforts, or think of a million new ways that you can fail.

The ironic thing about attracting Energy Angels into your life is that you need to focus on yourself, rather than on others. If you become someone who gives off positive vibrations, who seems to have an endless store of energy that you can share... then you will attract others who are just like you. So the key is to master how to give away energy, in the certainty that you will get back more than you donate.

As the quote above suggests, this is a lot to do with self-esteem. Unless you respect yourself, and see yourself as worthy and capable of giving out positive energy, others won't be able to see you in a positive light either.

You might think that giving away energy is more likely to attract vampires than angels. To a certain extent this is true, so watch out! Don't give others all your time, energy and precious emotional support if you sense that this is a one-way street. You'll instinctively know if that's the case.

On the other hand, Energy Vampires are actually more likely to seek out or inadvertently find others of their own kind, who they can sit around with discussing how bad things have become.

So go forth and give energy, and feel waves of it come crashing back your way!

Chapter 23
Spend a day serving others

What does it mean, to serve others? It sounds suspiciously pious — a little bit self-righteous. But we believe that serving others can seriously energise your mind, body and spirit. The reasons why altruism is energising aren't particularly noble either — and they certainly aren't 'religious'.

Why does it feel good to do good?

The habit of only thinking of ourselves is ultimately energy-sapping. The problem is that we already know so much about ourselves that we can go on making finer and finer distinctions about our characters, motives, habits, objectives and dreams. This means that energy is spent on navel gazing, and not really getting out there and achieving something.

So spending a day serving others is all about liberation from the things that hold you back and stop you using your energy. To constantly look inwards and be concerned about yourself is like putting up huge hurdles that stop you from running freely. You may get lost in your own thoughts, and obsessed by details. Contrast this with what happens when you decide to serve others.

First you'll notice a newfound perspective that was lost through focussing exclusively on your own problems. You may find that the challenges that other people face are actually much more significant than your own. It's inspiring to realise that some people not only have more serious problems than us, but they also deal with them better than we do. Pity turns to admiration for people who have real issues to deal with.

We need to be careful about our own motives when we serve others. If you're helping people to look good, to be admired, to appear heroic, then eventually you'll be found out. There's a special kind of energy that comes from helping others anonymously, without thought of reward. Wayne Dyer tells a great story about anonymously putting money into other people's parking meters so they don't get a ticket!

So what are the practicalities of serving others?

The purpose of this exercise isn't to store up rewards in the afterlife, or to be admired while we're on earth. It's just a special way of increasing our energy and freeing our ability to use it. The quality and quantity of the act of service isn't particularly important — what you're aiming to do is put the ego in its place, to move yourself from the centre of your own thoughts, and to stop being obsessive about the details of your own problems.

It isn't required that you establish a new charity bringing relief to the poor. You don't need to devote your whole life to working with an impoverished community. Although these are no doubt wonderful and noble things to do, they are not for everyone. If you aren't one of that special breed who devote their lives to good causes, there are easier ways to contribute to others and simultaneously free the energy being suppressed by your own self-absorption.

The important thing is simply to increase your own awareness of what is happening around you. Sometimes people are served by a few kind words, and no actions are needed. On some occasions there's a physical effort needed to help — but this can be as simple as helping a young mother struggling with her buggy and young child to negotiate some stairs. Think about the symbolism of that for a moment, about what is really going on below the surface. You can walk by, or you can spend a few seconds on assisting someone to overcome an obstacle. You are at the apex of a pyramid of capability — the young child who cannot walk, the mother who cannot negotiate the stairs quickly enough to catch the train that's waiting on the station — and you, who have the energy and strength to create a good outcome.

Imagine for a moment how you feel if you walk by the situation. The memory lingers, if only for moments. Sheepish guilt, energy-sapping regret and painful self-consciousness. Now imagine if you had helped in that situation. You move on, you forget it, you take the energy you gained from forgetting about your own problems, and you use that to stride out into whatever the rest of the day brings you! It's childishly simple, it's no big deal, and it won't change the world.

Will it?

Chapter 24
Finding Energy Angels

The best and surest way of finding Energy Angels is to freely give your energy, to be optimistic, vivacious, forward looking and cheerful. That way, you'll attract other people into your life who are just like you.

Do you know any Energy Angels? Who makes you feel good? Who makes you smile? Seek out *their* company.

Who would you turn to in times of trouble? Who is always there for you, before you have to ask?

There are two kinds of Energy Angels. The first are usually very easy to spot—they're the ones who love and support you!

These people though, aren't necessarily close personal friends. They're the kind of people who just naturally have temperaments that lead them to nurture, support, encourage and motivate. They would as soon put you down or undermine you as live underwater. Being upbeat and encouraging is like breathing for them.

We can make a finer distinction about these kinds of nurturing, supportive people. There are different ways to be 'upbeat' in life, and not all Energy Angels have huge beaming smiles and cheer-leading voices. Is it possible to be mildly introverted and still be an Energy Angel? Absolutely. In fact, the people who give quiet, insightful encouragement are often the most positive influences in our lives.

Now on to the second type of Energy Angel. This kind can be a bit harder to spot. The good they're doing to us isn't always so obvious. That's because they aren't necessarily even aware of our existence, let alone consciously trying to give us energy. But when you think about other ways that you receive energy—by soaking in the sun, eating healthy foods, breathing in the positive energy to be found near the ocean—it's obvious that these sources don't have our well-being as a conscious aim. The sun shines because it shines. There may well be a grand hidden design behind it, but the sun isn't consciously nurturing us. It just happens.

So it is with the second kind of Energy Angel. They give out energy just because they give out energy. Then how do we recognise them?

Energy Angel #2 is very often obsessed with something — but never with him or herself. These people are impassioned, incredibly knowledgeable, and inspire us by the way in which they see beauty in the most unlikely places. We know one man who is an unacknowledged expert on Georgian architecture. He is unacknowledged because his interest exists in and of itself, not so that he can be famous amongst other people who share the same interests. In fact, he avoids such people on the whole, because they tend to transform a passion into a hobby... a more pallid version of the same thing.

The man we have in mind looks at a Georgian building and sees a work of art, a history, and a living process; he looks at bricks and mortar and understands the toil, sweat and love that went into making each brick perfect, and each recipe for mortar unique to the area in which it was made, using local materials. Buildings become epics, sagas, symbols of a time when craftsmanship was paramount, and care and skill were developed over lifetimes.

This is just one example, but it brings to mind another interesting trait of Energy Angel #2. He or she is very often idiosyncratic and unconventional. They inspire us not just by showing us beauty where we hadn't noticed it before, but by showing us that life itself can be inspirational and unique. They show us that it's possible to find our own ways of doing things.

One final trait is worth noting. The unconventional energy angels who go through life following their passions, are very unlikely to admit the possibility — let alone the reality — of failure. This is not necessarily because they're arrogant, but because they live by their own yardsticks. They experiment and note the results, and are driven on by their passions to experiment again. This is life—it isn't 'failure'!

Thank God for unconventional people!

Chapter 25
Do the spiritual spring cleaning

As we suggested before, you will attract into life things and people that are just like you. So if you give out masses of energy — you'll get masses back. And if you are a lover of life, life will love you and nurture you.

That may sound to you like the worst kind of Pollyanna new age gibberish, designed for people who are already comfortable in their lives, except that they need something simple to believe in. As with so many other things in this book though, we don't ask you to believe it — we just ask you to try it. Experience has shown that this is how things work.

Most of us have episodes from the past that prevent us from being positive and energetic. The memory and the sub-conscious store up past events, feelings and reactions that may be real or imaginary, and these act like brakes on our energy, creativity and sheer exuberance. Some people even hold keepsakes of negative memories. Throw them away now!

So this chapter is about taking care of unfinished business, and about cleaning the windows of our perception of all the messy stuff that's built up over the years.

Imagine the energy that you generate as a beam of pure light that gets dimmed and diffused by filters that your own mind puts in the way. Those filters are the doubts, insecurities and destructive obsessions of your ego, damaged by past events and current difficulties. If you could remove those filters, your energy would shine like a laser. Let's quickly run through the kinds of filters you may have put in the way of your natural source of energy.

The single most distorting filter is probably the inability to let go of past hurts and insults. Because of the way the sub-conscious works, feelings of resentment, revenge and hatred can attach themselves to events of great importance on the one hand, or on the other the tiniest slight or insult that the perpetrator probably wasn't even aware of. The way to remove the filter is the same in both cases, and it's called 'forgiveness'.

Some of the things that have been done to us are truly terrible, and a feeling of a need for revenge could probably be justified on moral or even legal grounds. But the fact is that forgiveness is not something you do for the benefit of the person who has hurt you — it's something you do for yourself. Resentment is a load that *you* carry — not your tormentor. That person has moved on. So forgiveness is something you owe *yourself*.

We often hear people say "I can forgive, but I can never forget". Why not? Far better to forget too. Move on, leave it all behind, lost in the past where it should be. Set yourself free from those who have hurt you. You're bigger and better than attachments to a painful past would have you be.

The next energy filters that you can remove are related to acceptance and rejection. Sometimes we feel ourselves limited in what we can achieve by factors outside of our control. This dims our energy to an enormous extent. But there are two kinds of limitations and your reactions to them should be entirely different.

The first kind of limitation is 'natural'. It may be that you would like to be the fastest runner in the world, but no matter how hard you train and do all the things needed to improve your speed, you are never going to be the fastest runner, due to your genetic make-up. You were made for other things.

Your response to this shouldn't be one of resentment or prolonged disappointment, but one of *acceptance*. You need to exercise care with this though, because there are millions of stories of the triumph of the human spirit over apparent limitations. Don't accept second best because it's easy or you've been told to. Perhaps the limits of the possible have been drawn too tightly around your life. But if you are absolutely sure that you have a limitation that cannot be overcome — accept it and move on. You are being given a sign that you were actually made for bigger and better things.

On the other hand, there are apparent limitations to our possibilities which are invented and imposed by other human beings, politics and social conventions. Reject them all. Some people may be hurt by your success in overcoming limitations that they are imprisoned by. They would like you to stay in prison with them, not break out and find your own freedom. That's their problem, not yours.

As for political realities—change them if necessary. The twentieth century is full of great examples for you to draw on, where the supposed truth of political realities was overcome by men and women who refused to accept chains, inequality and injustice.

Social conventions? These are subtle prisons that should be torn down. This doesn't excuse anyone from basic good manners—we could do with more charm in the world, not less. But you do have a right to reject limitations imposed upon you by attitudes to your class, gender, age, religion, race, nationality or other artificial barrier to achievement. *It shall not stand.* Reject it!

There's another aspect to acceptance and rejection. This is to do with accepting your own foibles, idiosyncrasies, and deviations from the norm. You don't need to shoe-horn yourself into an acceptable mould, though it sometimes seems like the pressure to conform increases every day. When you can accept yourself, you can accept others too. When you can accept yourself, and love who you are, your energy can shine—unfiltered.

Chapter 26
Inspire someone!

Being an inspiration for other people is straightforward, once you have the key to doing it. It will increase your energy and that of the person you inspire, and both of you will skip through the rest of the day.

You may be surprised by the idea that inspiring someone is easy. When we think of inspirational people, we tend to think of great heroes and heroines, brave people who have ventured into unknown territory, or bravely overcome seemingly insurmountable odds. If you are one of those, all well and good. Maybe your presence alone is enough to inspire, because when people think of you, they think of your history and achievements.

As an inspirational speaker, Jo motivates and helps people all over the world with her story-telling. It's true that her stories aren't exactly run of the mill — it's not every day you meet the Royal Air Force's first female Fighter Pilot — but the key to Jo's speaking is to be able to relate these exceptional circumstances to every-day reality. The same principles apply to small challenges as apply to big ones. Courage, confidence, determination and energy are called for in most challenges worth the name.

There's also a way to inspire people that doesn't require heroism. Many people go through days, weeks and months of their lives without the experience of another human being listening to them and taking a genuine interest. Listening to someone is one of the most inspiring things that you can do. In fact, once you have developed listening skills you will see that it's the first stage of a simple five step process that will help you to inspire others. Those steps are...

> Listen
>> Believe
>>> Challenge
>>>> Structure and
>>>>> Expect

Let's look at each of these in turn, remembering that inspiring someone is an art, not a science. Once you have the hang of it, you'll internalise the process and the five steps will become part of your intuitive ability to inspire others. So, *Listening* first…

When you really listen to someone, you aren't worried about an awkward silence arising. If you were worried about that, your thoughts would start to wander towards what you are going to say when it's your turn to speak. That would mean that in fact you would no longer be listening, but going round and round in your own thoughts. Your ego would be fretting about how you can appear to be wise and sympathetic. So listening is about the other person — not you! It takes some bravery to let go of your ego and just listen.

The best way to be wise is to be innocent. By 'innocent', I mean that our only response when truly listening is to ask genuinely interested questions to try to understand the issues at hand. But how can quietly listening, asking interested questions, and not worrying about giving wise advice, possibly inspire the other person? This takes us to the second step of the process.

The person who needs or is looking for inspiration, already knows at some level the answer to whatever issue she's tackling. Your listening intently to her will encourage her to unearth answers and tactics and strategies as she talks. She will uncover successful strategies which were laying dormant in the subconscious the whole time. However, for this process to happen, *you have to believe that the person in front of you has both the ability and the skills to solve the problem for herself.*

Armed with this belief in the other person, you won't be tempted to rush to your own solution to what is for them a very personal issue. And by your skilfully allowing her to find her own answers, based on your belief that she is wise, capable and intelligent, you increase your friend's self-esteem and confidence in a way that could never have been achieved if you simply came up with a pat answer.

On the other hand, you also need to be prepared to *challenge* someone in need of inspiration. Expect the absolute best of others. Do not accept their timidity or complacency.

You don't have to be rude in the way you challenge someone, but you may have to take that person to an uncomfortable place. Don't forget that although you are sure your friend can uncover her own solutions, she may be temporarily blinded to the truth. Maybe she can't see the wood for the trees, and you are the person who is able to offer a new perspective on things. This is the nature of challenging to inspire — you tell it like it is.

The fourth step in the process is to offer structure. Now that both of you have a good idea of the issues, and a new perspective on them, what is actually going to get done? Ask directly of anyone you wish to inspire: what's the plan? What are you aiming to do, and by when? What's your first step?

Another nice touch to add in is to ask the other person how committed she is to achieving the aims she's just outlined. Look out for body language as well as words, and if your friend isn't wholeheartedly committed to her course of action, it's unlikely she will carry it out. If that's the case — there must be a reason for it, which you can choose to help to uncover by once again challenging her.

The final step in the process is one of *expecting* the other person to not only do what they said they would do, but to do it wonderfully, successfully, in the most stellar fashion possible. This is another aspect of your faith in the ability of others. Transmit to them your confidence and expectation. Don't use heavy language that transforms everything into yet another task on an already crowded to-do list. Just let your friend know that you'll be waiting to hear what happens, but that of course you already know that they'll succeed!

Part 6

✻

Tapping into Universal Energy

Just as there is no loss of basic energy in the universe, so no thought or action is without its effects, present or ultimate, seen or unseen, felt or unfelt.

Norman Cousins

This section is where we really have some fun. It's all about how to extract energy from the most unlikely places.

Let your guard down to let in some new ideas—you have nothing to lose and huge amounts of energy to gain. Western readers aren't used to some of the strange and wonderful knowledge about energy that's been around in other cultures for centuries, and which we're now going to use.

The very air you breathe is full of energy, and all you have to do is use your mind to tap into it. Trees, bushes and water are great sources of energy, if you know how to approach them. There are Power Places where you can feed on an invisible energy that will sustain your spirit, enthuse your mind and power your body. The sun is a powerhouse of energy for you to use.

Come with us on this journey and enjoy it. If you take some of these things to heart, you'll have great fun, or life changing experiences, or even better—both.

Try these things out for size, have a great time, and tune into Universal Energy.

Chapter 27
Tap into the energy that's everywhere

What did you look like, before you had a face?

This is a question taken from the Zen tradition. It's an invitation to consider your origins.

When did you 'start'?

There's something walking around the earth with your name and your features attached to it. Through the miracle of consciousness that 'something' identifies that name and those features as itself. It's convinced that it exists in time and space! But when did that 'something' take on its own existence?

The answer can't be *"My existence started when I was born"* or *"When I began to develop recognisably human features in the womb"*. That would not make sense. You are not born out of nothingness. You are born as the result of sperm penetrating an ovum. So what were you, before that penetration and eventual development of something recognisably human?

Well, now we have two paths to follow — that of the sperm, or that of the ovum! And we can keep on following the paths back in time, and down into microscopic cells and atomic and sub-atomic realms, looking for the source. But both paths lead to the same place. You came from a field where there is only Energy, and where there is some process or intention to have that field of energy manifest itself in ways that are visible and three dimensional.

It isn't only conscious humans who emanate from the field of Energy. It's true of everything we see — rocks, trees, and stars in the depths of space. It's all an expression of an underlying field of energy.

If this is true, then everything around us is made of the same energy. We're walking through an energy field which has intended our existence, and that of everything and every being around us. How marvellous!

Of all the things that are in existence in this energy field, one of the most subtle, mysterious and difficult to understand is the Mind itself.

Like everything else around us, Mind is a manifestation of a unified field of energy. However, Mind is special because it shares so many of the characteristics of its own source — the field of energy itself.

First of all, it's apparently invisible and undetectable by other senses or scientific instruments. Although we can examine the properties of things that seem to come along with it — such as chemical reactions in the brain — we cannot examine it directly. Secondly, Mind has intention, and is conscious of its own existence (a property we can imagine that the field of energy has, or else why would the Universe around us be in existence?).

There's a theory that Mind and the universal energy field are one and the same thing, and that individual human minds are simply tiny, self-conscious parts of a much greater whole. One can imagine again a drop of water rising as condensation from the ocean, falling again as rain onto the earth, joining with other drops to form streams and rivers that return to the ocean. At various points in the cycle, the drop of water seems to have an independent existence. But its stability and separateness is an illusion. It only exists as part of a system.

Our individual human minds are essential in manipulating energy in our lives — they're connected to that energy, can summon it, direct it and be a part of it. Our minds are like the drops of water that form the bigger system — but unlike those drops, individual minds can grasp the totality of the system, then use that understanding to reconnect with the greater Mind, which in turn is the source of all energy.

Over the next few chapters we'll look at the practical benefits of all this. These are not our inventions, but the results of thousands of years of study, practise and refinement. No doubt there are many more ways of tapping into Universal Energy, but these are just a few of the ways that we've found effective.

For now, just act as though you're connected to the great source of energy that you came from and to which you will return. You are part of the energy that generates every aspect of reality.

What if you could use all this energy? What would that feel like? How would your body and mind feel, knowing that you are part of this huge all-powerful system?

Feel the energy coursing through your mind and body. Tap into the power, and feel that you're able to generate your own reality, with your own power. Be conscious of the Universe and your part in it. Be prepared for some fascinating and even more powerful techniques!

Chapter **28**

More on using the breath to generate energy

If you're aware of the Universal Mind and source of energy, and maybe see your journey here on earth as part of a cycle of leaving and returning to the source, here's a question with a new dimension to it.

What is your breath?

Perhaps the breath is our connection to the Unified Field of energy, the underlying source of everything that we are, can sense and can know. When you know the techniques that help you to concentrate on the breath, you can think about this connection with the universe with each breath you take.

First let's concentrate on the easiest way to use the breath in relation to energy. This is more about conserving energy than generating it, but the overall effect is the same.

One of the most common ways to waste energy is to have it sapped by our own out-of-control thoughts, the kind that go spinning around our heads, sometimes for hours and even days, on a tight loop that repeats over and over. Sometimes when we become aware that this is happening, it can lead us to think that we've been close to insanity—completely unable to control our thoughts, and therefore our actions. Even worse is when we *don't* realise that this is what's happening.

Recent research has revealed that large numbers of people think more or less the same thoughts today as they did yesterday. Just think about that one for a moment! Not only are we quietly obsessed with something that is grabbing our attention (and our energy), but we are failing to move on. We are reproducing today, exactly that which got us nowhere yesterday. Of course, there are exceptions when this can be productive—when, for instance, we are going back over difficult technical problems which we need to put serious thought into. But most repeating patterns aren't like that—they are noisy, self-destructive and negative, and drive out useful, creative thinking.

So the first thing to do is quieten the mind—and this is where control of the breath comes into its own. These methods will help you to 'stop the bleeding' of your energy that happens when your thought patterns move in vicious circles.

In the exercise that follows, read through once first, then go back and do each step.

Technique!
Using the Breath to Calm the Mind

- ✔ Sit in a comfortable chair, in a restful place where you won't be disturbed. Eventually, you'll be able to use the same techniques anywhere, and in many situations. For this exercise, close your eyes.
- ✔ Be aware of your breath as you inhale and exhale gently through your nostrils. Feel the sensation of the air rushing past the tip of your nose, into the naval cavity, down into your lungs, then back up warmly through your nose.
- ✔ Follow the passage of air with your attention, without thoughts. When thoughts arise, there is no need to struggle with them. Simply let them go, gently and peacefully.
- ✔ When disturbing thoughts arise, don't beat yourself up about allowing your negative thought patterns to take over; just let go of them, and return gently to following your breath as it moves past your nostrils.

- ✔ Count the number of breath cycles, starting with an inhalation, and counting 'one' (quietly, in the mind) with the first exhalation. Try to do this ten times, with a still mind in between each count. Amongst other things, this will show you just how hard it can be to control your own mind! With practice it will strengthen your will power enormously.

Try changing the patterns of inhalation and exhalation. There are many of these, which you can gently experiment with. Here are just a few. Don't try them all at once — spend a week or two on each one, being sensitive to the changes brought about in your energy levels, thoughts and feelings.

Technique!

Rhythmic Breathing Patterns

Read through once first, then go back and do each step.

- ✔ Inhale as you silently count, then gently exhale to a silent count.
- ✔ Be aware of the ratio between your inhalations and exhalations. For instance, you may be inhaling for a count of five, then exhaling to a count of ten (a 1:2 ratio).
- ✔ Gradually, increase the count as you inhale, breathing deeply into the bottom of your lungs, feeling your abdomen swelling (not your chest) as the lungs press down on the diaphragm.

- ✔ Now, increase the count as you exhale in the same ratio. So if you breathe in to a count of 8 and the ratio is 1:2, exhale to a count of 16.
- ✔ Feel that you are pushing out all of the expended breath from your lungs. Only go as far as is comfortable, in a way that allows your mind to remain still.

You can change this rhythmic breathing pattern to include holding your breath, as follows.

Rhythmic Breathing with Breath Retention

Read through once first, then go back and do each step.

- ✔ Inhale for a count of five, hold the breath for a count of five, then exhale for a count of ten.
- ✔ Adjust the counts so that you are comfortable, but try to keep the ratio the same.
- ✔ For example, instead of 5:5:10, you could try 4:4:8. Gradually increase the counts though, keeping the ratio identical.

These breathing patterns can induce a deep sense of calm and wellbeing. It's important not to strain or feel uncomfortable, and to let the mind be still. **When you have mastered these, use great care in trying the following:**

> ## Rhythmic Breathing with Breath Retention and Empty Lungs
>
> Read through once first, then go back and do each step.
>
> **· If at any time you feel dizzy, or in any way uncomfortable, gently return to normal breathing.**
>
> - ✔ Inhale to a count of four
> - ✔ Hold the breath to a count of four
> - ✔ Exhale to a count of eight
> - ✔ Hold the lungs empty to a count of four.
> - ✔ You can shorten or lengthen the counts, but keep them in the same ratio of: 1:1:2:1.

These are great ways of conserving energy and increasing your capacity to generate it. But what about actually using the breath to generate energy?

Once more, it's all in the relationship between the breath and the mind, these two mysterious and powerful forces that underlie our existence. In the earlier exercises, you focused on making the mind quiet; now you will use the mind to *increase energy*.

Technique!
Using the Breath to Generate Energy

Read through once first, then go back and do each step.

- ✔ Sit in a comfortable chair, in a restful place where you won't be disturbed. Close your eyes.
- ✔ Place the soles of the feet on the floor, and the palms of the hands upwards, resting in your lap.
- ✔ As you breathe in, silently know that you breathe in pure energy.
- ✔ Feel the energy coursing through your torso and limbs, making your fingers and toes tingle with the crackling power of life.
- ✔ As you breathe out, know that you send enormous energy out into the world.
- ✔ Feel the positive feedback loop, as the energy increases with every breath. Feel yourself to be a powerful energy generator.

As you come back quietly to the room you're in, carry your energy out into the world, and use it to accomplish your dreams today. Perhaps you have a job interview, a speech to give, or a difficult job to get through. Now you have the energy!

Chapter **29**

Drawing energy from nature... tree huggers unite!

Now that you know how to use the breath to conserve and generate energy while you sit comfortably in your own home or familiar environment, you can amplify the effects by taking these techniques outside.

The Chinese have the marvellous idea that the energy coursing through our bodies is the very same energy that's all around us in the sky, the trees and the sun, and even in rocks and other inanimate objects. This is why in China you can see masses of people exercising outside in the fresh air. Chi Kung and Tai Chi are exercise systems that draw energy from nature, and they are well worth learning from a good teacher. But there are some basic principles that you can take on board right now. If you find them beneficial, find a good teacher of one of the ancient physical arts of China, and embark on a lifetime of discovery of your connection to the energies of nature.

We've adapted these simple exercises, and used what works most powerfully for us.

Find a quiet place in a park, or a garden, or in a wilder part of nature, preferably where you won't be disturbed. Do this before the sun gets too hot, in the early morning. Either face the sun so it shines on your face, or turn around and expose as much of your naked back to its rays as you can. The small of the back is a special place on the body, able to soak up the energy of the sun.

Remove your shoes and socks. Feel the earth beneath you. Be aware of the dew on the soles of your feet, or the dryness of the dust. As you quieten your mind and become aware of your breath, let your weight sink down through your knees, through the soles of your feet, and into the earth. Feel yourself rooted like a huge oak. Let all stiffness fade from your body and especially your joints. Unlock your knees and elbows.

Be aware of your breath, feel the sun on your skin and how its energy enters your body through your skin and your breath. As you breathe in, feel the energy of the sky and sun flowing through you. Let the energy rush out through the soles of your feet, down into the earth as you breathe out.

This time, as you breathe in, raise your arms slowly to the sky in a big, open gesture of welcome and acceptance. Completing the circle, lower your arms gently as you breathe out. You will feel balanced, strong, light and energetic.

Here's another one you can try. Stand close by a tree or bush. Look for a specimen that suits you and is energetic—you don't have to think about what this means—at some level you already know. The Chinese believe that evergreens and flowering bushes have particularly powerful energy... so you might want to experiment with those.

As you breathe in, feel that you're drawing energy up through the earth from the roots of the tree beneath you. As you exhale, feel the energy flowing through your head and fingers and heart, out through the air, and into the tree or bush through its leaves and branches. Feel the energy moving in a great circle through yourself and the tree. Imagine that you're part of the same living organism, sharing energy, strength and power through the breath and the mind. Accept this for what it is.

Finally, here's another breathing exercise that is even easier, and only one step above laying on the beach!

The idea of 'power places' comes from Native American cultures. The idea is that there are places, possibly unique to you, where you can harvest enormous amounts of energy. For some people, these places might be by the sea or on a hilltop. For instance, in hilly areas you can sometimes find huge slabs of rock that sit in the sun all day and, like storage heaters, give up their energy when you lay on them, under an evening sky, surrounded by all the energy-giving elements of nature. Lay with a quiet mind, carried on the back of a slab of rock connected to the earth, hurtling through the space of our solar system, a tiny speck of mind and breath in a Universe of Energy.

Chapter 30
Experience something beautiful today

People who have masses of energy find the time to experience beauty in their lives on a daily basis. Maybe you've been advised to do this before but the advice just didn't take. 'Make sure you catch the sunset today' someone might say. Or, 'Walk in the park — it's lovely at this time of year'.

It's hard to take that kind of advice when you're stressed, under pressure or absorbed in the problems of the day. These are exactly the times when your friends know that you need to re-charge your batteries.

When you're under pressure though, you can't see the wood for the trees. Advice like this can seem irrelevant, annoyingly naive and idealistic. Perhaps your head is down, you're in the waking sleep of self-obsession, dealing with the current crisis and moving on to the next one. Too numbed by pressing issues to be able to wake up and smell the roses.

Is this where you are now? What's your reaction to people who advise you to rest or slow down? If you are typically frustrated and annoyed that they can't see your reality, if you are thinking 'if only they knew what life was like for me and how pathetic that advice is', then this is probably the time in your life when you are most in need of that advice! Admit the possibility that your view of the world may be skewed, and that others have a perspective that in your current circumstances you just can't see. That's a big step, resisted strongly by your ego, which always knows best. But try taking that step and then see what happens from there.

When someone asks you to 'make sure you see something beautiful today' you may take this to mean a certain kind of beauty that's very difficult to find if you live in one of the biggest, dirtiest, noisiest and most over-crowded cities in the world. But there are different kinds of beauty and sources of energy all around us — and you can tap into them at any time.

An urban sunset can be every bit as spectacular and peaceful as watching the sun sink into the ocean, surrounded by nature, silence and wheeling gulls. The sun and sky are above everything on earth, even the most frantic city on earth. The key though is to realise that you can find beauty not just in the natural world, and not just through your visual senses. There's a whole world in a grain of sand — it's just a question of quieting your mind for long enough to pay attention to the beauty and meaning that's all around you.

There are recordings by artists who use the sounds they find around them to create patterns and 'soundscapes'. They use people's voices, or the sounds of traffic, or a few notes of a refrain sung by an old man or a child, and then transform these into creations of amazing beauty, using the wonderful technology available today. When you realise the possibilities of this, suddenly the sense of hearing becomes dominant. The attention is focused on qualities of sound rather than the appearances of everything and the world is transformed. Voices form patterns, weaving gold through a tapestry of sound that includes the cries of birds, the sounds of traffic, the whistle and mighty sighs of wind, and the creaking of trees. On and on this new world goes, an unexplored and ever changing landscape, a source of fascination and wonder that is every bit as beautiful as a sunset.

The point is that a shift in attention can have a great effect on our appreciation of everything around us. Sights, smells, sounds, tastes and feelings can become sources of great energy. We *do* know how to focus our attention on these things, but for some reason we don't. We forget. We need someone to jolt us out of our habitual patterns of perception so that we can wake up and smell the coffee, hear the delight in a stranger's voice, feel the breeze ruffling the hairs on our arms, taste the food in our mouths, and see the new dawn.

Chapter 31
A Day full of quality

How much of your day is spent on *Autopilot*? Do whole parts of your life go missing? Sometimes it's hard to tell one day from another, and to remember the difference between, let's say, Tuesday and Thursday of last week. Is this because our lives are inherently boring and uneventful?

Many people find meaning, delight and energy in every moment—and yet, externally their lives are neither exciting nor glamorous. What it boils down to is attention to the moment you're in right now. You can flood this moment with colour, you can find the magic in it, and you can savour every detail of the life you're living. You don't need to bungee jump to do this—you just need to practice being in the moment.

Some people need to overcome feelings of worthlessness before they can really live in the moment. They believe that "my life isn't anything special". Living profoundly means recognising that your life is as important as anyone else's—you're an expression of the same life force and field of energy, whether you are a road sweeper or a President.

Once we can accept that we're living a life that matters, no matter how obscure or troubled, the world slows down to a speed where we can catch it. Imagine that! Think of slowing down the world so that you can gently catch it in your awareness, and examine it at your leisure in all its beauty and fine detail.

The Japanese Tea Ceremony is an example of this kind of thinking. It's a social occasion where attention to the tiniest of details of the ritual symbolise the fact that it's unique. It can never be repeated in exactly the same way again. Each moment is special and can be lived to the full—*must* be lived to the full, or else it's gone, like a rainbow that hung above you in the sky, but which you didn't notice because you had your head down.

The details of the Tea Ceremony ritual are meaningful in themselves. It doesn't matter for our purposes what the exact symbolism is. We just need to look at this situation and relate it to ourselves and how we live. What we see is someone preparing and serving tea. Every gesture has its beauty and its meaning. It's done slowly and mindfully. There is no thinking about other things, while the physical body carries out pre-programmed instructions. The body and the mind are one. There is only this experience, now, and the person who lives it is not split in two by thinking one thing and doing another.

Try slowing down the world today. It's good for the soul.

Of course, you don't have to indulge in any kind of ritual, let alone the Tea Ceremony itself, to slow down the world and live days full of quality. The point is to bring your mind to everything that you do—to focus on the task in hand and perform it with perfection.

This is not the same thing as 'get on with it' or 'achieve more' or 'don't procrastinate'. What we're after is quality, not necessarily quantity. Try starting this through observation, first of others, then of yourself. When you observe others, you'll see that much activity is done while people are 'asleep'. There are automatic responses to automatic stimuli, and the words you hear are often stock phrases bandied about to ease everyone through the day without too much fuss. There's a sense of ritual here too, but it is ritual carried out while sleep-walking.

When you observe yourself and your own actions closely, a strange thing happens.

You wake up.

The very act of bringing the attention to what you're saying and doing has the effect of bringing alive the senses, of making you aware of all the wonders around you, the sights, sounds, feelings, smells and tastes. This is amazingly energising, and once you're that wide awake, you can deal with the quality of your own actions, and carry out your business with skill, grace and care.

If these ideas are new to you, it's possible that you don't recognise that much of our activity in the world is done while 'sleep-walking'. Consider the possibility that the reason for your doubt is that you may be asleep!

Or you may imagine that to stay awake, to bring your attention to each moment, is an easy thing. If that's true for you, then you are very fortunate. For most people it takes great effort. We get caught in the nets of our own thoughts, lost in the intricate passages of the mind, while meanwhile the world rushes past.

This brings us back around to the Tea Ceremony. These kinds of rituals do have an important purpose, and that's to help the participants to be mindful. The catch is that the opposite can occur, and tasks that are too familiar are easy to do without really thinking. The answer is to bring awareness to each action, and be aware of its quality. For instance, walk across the room, from this side to that... what is the best, the most graceful or energetic way of doing that?

There are another couple of techniques that help to bring attention to the quality of our actions. The first is one that we're familiar with – become aware of your breathing. Focus on it as you move around. The inner peace produced allows you to become aware of your connection to everything around you.

Living in London, one of the most obvious places where people sleep-walk is on the Tube. For the most part we're not conscious of one another – or all *too* conscious as we try to not get crushed in the rush hour. In such a crowded place sometimes your eyes may meet a stranger's gaze. This is not a coincidence. It is a special moment. In Hinduism, the Namaste gesture (bringing together the palms of the hands with a slight bow) is said to acknowledge the holiness of the person being greeted. So when your eyes meet another's, recognise that you are both part of something bigger. With an almost imperceptible smile and nod of the head, recognise the bond between you.

Finally, there's an attitude towards our own actions that will help sharpen awareness. This is simply the idea that we should be impeccable in our behaviour and fastidious in our actions. Being impeccable and fastidious doesn't mean that you need to be stiff or militaristic. It just means that you can be conscious of your actions in a way that creates self-confidence and strength, that produces results of quality, and that generates massive energy.

Chapter 32
Walk in nature

This chapter is about all the ways that you can energise yourself by walking in nature. If you're like many Western people with a sedentary life style, just the act of walking will do you good, get the blood pumping, and whet your appetite for more.

But no matter how good walking is for you, that isn't what this chapter is really about. You can become energised in nature by using your mind and body to become aware of everything that's around you.

Nature reminds us of just how tiny and insignificant we are in relation to everything around us. Try being near the ocean on a day when the wind is whipping up, clouds are gathering on the horizon, and a few miles out to sea a storm is brewing and heading your way. The deep swells gather and break, the surf starts to churn, and you become aware of the enormous power of nature. Your own life is put into perspective. You're able to see yourself as a part of a much grander scheme of things which doesn't have *you* at its centre.

Compared to some life forms, it may seem that human consciousness is sophisticated and advanced. But when we stand before a wild ocean, we get the liberating sense that life is a simpler affair than we had imagined, with huge energetic forces in play across the Earth and the Universe, before which we stand neither dominant nor puny, but just connected.

Try looking at the sky — and particularly the night sky. If you walk along a country road on a late summer evening, miles from any human settlements or electric light, the brightness of even a half-moon is remarkable, illuminating the landscape and lighting the path. With the visual senses dampened by the half-light, the other senses kick in, and you begin to sense a different kind of night life — the busy goings on of small mammals in the hedgerows, owls calling, the summer breeze making music through the trees, every species producing different notes like huge instruments rooted in the earth.

Try lying down on a gently sloping hillside on a cloudless night. Become aware that looking at the stars is a way of looking into the past. The light that reaches your eyes started on its journey many years before. Perhaps some of the stars you're looking at no longer exist, so far away that their light has taken millennia to reach the earth. You realise that all experience is in the past — that people speak to you in their present, but there is a delay before you hear them. Perhaps all that's really available to you in the present are your own thoughts.

These are the kinds of ideas that can come up when we open ourselves to nature.

There's another aspect of nature which is energising and motivating. At first it may seem morbid, but hang on in there.

Natural processes play out over long periods of time, such as the cycle of the seasons, or the formation of the earth. On the other hand, there's the transience of so much in nature — the life cycle of a mayfly for instance. There's another way of saying this, which is that everywhere we look in life, we find death. Things arise, and disappear.

Where does the span of a normal life fit into the seemingly infinite stretch of time? We are little more than mayflies. We're gone almost as soon as we arrived, a little bit of consciousness in a sea of time, like plankton in the ocean.

Some people may find that perspective depressing — but it can be really motivating. How short our time is! How little time there is to waste! This can be one of the most energising perspectives on life that you'll ever get. Like the animals we see pecked at by crows on the roadside, the flies that struggle in a spider's web, only to be wrapped in a silky death, we are destined to perish. And yet as puny as we are, we have free will, consciousness and the ability to change our behaviour. We can spend our time investigating this mystery of life, and live it with passion and energy!

Chapter **33**
Time Management

No doubt, you're starting to get the hang of the somewhat different take on things in this book, so the title of this chapter probably didn't fool you. We're not going to advise you to write lists, or to divide a piece of paper into four compartments where you can park your dreams for today. We have a different approach!

First of all though, let's deal with this subject of conventional time management so we can get it out of the way.

If you have a problem that you call 'time management'; or if you find yourself constantly looking for new ways to give priority to what you feel you must do; or if your life is full of lists then something is wrong with the way you're living your life!

The amazing thing is that lists in particular and Time Management in general are meant to be a way of maximising our productivity, but in fact *they do the opposite*.

So what is productivity? It's the subject of a field in economics. You are not a machine, you are a human being. And even if you accept that the idea of productivity is applicable to humans, you have to bear in mind that it's quality that counts, not quantity.

So why do we boldly state that traditional time management actually decreases productivity?

Sometimes we waste time on the list as a displacement activity. After all, there are lots of things you can do with lists—you can have daily, weekly and monthly lists, and roll those up into an annual set of objectives. You can divide the tasks by type: leisure, work, financial, etc; or by priority: urgent and important; not urgent but important; urgent but not important, and even not urgent and not important. When we do this, we honestly think we are doing something 'productive'. We are organising our thinking. We are being logical and rational in allotting time in such a way that we maximise the time we have. For instance, we don't drive into town to do task A, drive back home to do task B, and then back to town again for task C. We organise.

The problem with all this is that *it's obvious*. It gets us nowhere. You will *produce far more, and of much better quality, when you don't use traditional time management techniques.*

Let's look at the process.

When you get up in the morning it's blindingly obvious that there are things of vital importance that you should spend most of your energy on. There are other things rolling around at the back of your mind that you know need to be taken care of too, but you instinctively know that they aren't as important as the main event of the day. When they are as important, they'll stop rolling around at the back of your mind, and come to the forefront, and then you'll get them done.

Often, what comes to the forefront of the mind is very much what you *want* to do, rather than what you *need* to do. This has obvious drawbacks, but also some delightful consequences.

The advantage of doing what you really instinctively want to do, is that you come to it fresh, you come to it first (before your enthusiasm and energy has been tainted by doing all those things you *need* to do) and you come to it with happiness and energy. An example is writing this book. On a day when we don't have a list of things to do, this book gets written. We know that's it's really the thing we want to do, and that in the long term it's also actually the thing we need to do. We could have gone and made a list instead. That would have wasted some time almost without effort, and we would have felt good about getting so organised. First thing on the list would be to check our emails. Then of course someone would have sent a link to an interesting website, which we'll follow... and follow... and follow.

And on it goes. But today, we don't have a list. What we have is a body of writing!

Just to be clear about this, we're not suggesting that you don't have objectives. There's a famous piece of research that shows that people who write down their objectives far out-perform those who don't. No arguments here. But we do argue with the idea that our perception of each day we live — our image and symbol of it — is as a list of tasks. Your life is not a list of tasks — it's an adventure! It's a spiritual, intellectual, artistic creation that should defy description, pigeon-holing and even, occasionally, logic.

What is the underlying cause for using traditional Time Management techniques? Obviously, many people feel that they are drowning in too many tasks with too little time to carry them out. The theory is that reorganising the tasks by allotting them time will make some gain that otherwise wouldn't have been available. But there is no more time to be had, and the benefits of this reorganisation are lost in the time it takes to do it.

The underlying cause must surely be that you're doing too much and getting too little for it. Alternatively, you are not appreciating sufficiently what you do get as a reward for everything you do. If you already have a nice house and car, for instance, do you really want to push yourself yet harder so that you can get an even nicer one? Is this really where you get the juice from life? Or are you just caught up in the cycle of work and spending without fully realising it?

Here's a suggestion designed to give you energy to do what you want to do and what you need to do. It goes against the grain for many people. Experiment! See what happens! Are you sure your current system is getting you the results you want?

Tomorrow when you wake up, resist the urge to make a list of things to do. Listen to your instincts, your inner voice. Not the one that criticises and gets on your back and tells you the world will collapse if you don't get at least ten things done today. There's another voice that not only encourages you and supports you, it also fills you with energy. It even knows exactly what you should do. Listen out for it more and more, and start to follow where it leads.

The rest can wait.

Chapter 34
Gratitude

If you were born in the west into a society that's wealthy and at least reasonably caring about its citizens, how lucky you are! You were in the right place at the right time.

How incredible it is to have clean, running drinking water, right in our houses!

These are the things we take for granted, because they're just there. But sometimes it's good to step back and realise how much we really have. When we think of the world as an abundant place that supports us, it makes it easier to rise above whatever difficult circumstances we face. There's a rise in energy, and the feeling that anything is possible.

An "attitude of gratitude" is great for driving out feelings of 'poor disadvantaged me'. When we compare ourselves with others, we can always find things in our lives that are wonderful, and that we can be grateful for. Hot running water, a watertight roof over our heads, our health. Things that are so easy to take for granted. In fact though, we don't even need to compare ourselves with others. We are alive, aren't we? That in itself is a long shot, that we should be on earth with life coursing through our veins, and the chance to see what the fuss about being a human is all about. Once we realise we are not disadvantaged, but positively showered with gifts, we can start to take responsibility for what we do with the rest of our lives.

Gratitude helps us to focus on the positive aspects of life, and what we focus on is what we get. Tell yourself that you're lucky, powerful and wealthy, and you programme your mind to be just that. And luck, power and wealth is what you begin to attract.

If you don't know — in your bones — how lucky you are to have what you have, you'll enjoy it a lot less. You become complacent, satiated, over-full. Nothing can stimulate your pampered palate. Wayne Dyer, the motivational speaker and writer, talks about how the huge majority of the world's population can't take a shower in their homes (let alone have fresh water to drink). Now when I take a shower, I relish it, I savour it, and I love it.

Once you recognise what you have, and begin to really enjoy it, something else happens. You notice that there are things around you that don't really bring you any happiness. You have acquired things which may have cost a lot in time and effort, and yet, deep down, they don't make you any happier. Research has shown that beyond a certain point, extra wealth doesn't lead to extra happiness — in fact, sometimes quite the opposite. To be well fed and clothed with a roof over our heads is indeed a blessing — and as the saying goes, all the rest is gravy. So gratitude can be something that gives us balance, and lets us see clearly that our energy doesn't have to be squandered on things we don't really need for our happiness.

The psychologist Erich Fromm once asked a great question in the title of his book: *To Have or To Be?* Fromm recognised that consumers become like 'the eternal suckling, crying out for its bottle'. Being grateful for the things we already have can help us realise that we don't need to feel empty, that our energy and fulfilment comes from who we are, and not what we have.

Chapter **35**

The power of asking the universe for energy

> 1. Life is a struggle to the death. There isn't enough of anything to go around, so you have to fight to get your share. If you let up for a minute, you're in big trouble, and even if you do get wealthy, there's always someone trying to steal what you have.
>
> 2. The world is an abundant place. There's plenty of everything to go around—it's just a matter of attracting the right things into your life, and using your own skills and talents to find wealth and happiness.

This is the classic 'glass half empty or glass half full?' scenario. It's usually used to illustrate the two kinds of character predispositions that people have.

But it's more important than that, and here's why. First of all, we're taught that 'character predisposition' is written in stone and we can't change it. We're either optimists or pessimists and there's nothing we can do about that.

This simply isn't true. The way that you can prove it for yourself if you happen to be a 'glass half empty' kind of person, is to carry out an experiment. Even if you are an optimist and haven't tried this before, go for it... it is a fascinating exercise that can produce amazing results.

But first, a bit of background.

Imagine living life with the 'scarcity mentality'. You'd have to be on the lookout twenty four hours a day for an opportunity to grab any scarce resources you could find. Other people, because they're in competition with you, would essentially be your enemies. Either they get and you go without — or you get what's going and the devil take the hindmost. Over time, your character would change — you'd be untrusting and aggressive.

What kinds of people do you think you would attract into your life if this is how you carried on? The chances are that you'd attract people like yourself. It becomes a self-fulfilling prophecy. The people in your life would give you all the proof you need that existence is a tooth-and-nail struggle for scarce resources. They are aggressive, deceitful and determined to do you down. You have to be harder and more ruthless than they are which in turn will attract harder and more ruthless people.

Now imagine that you have an Abundance Mentality and the world is a place where there can be plenty for everyone. Chances are that you would be generous, open and relaxed. You'd be ready for opportunities when they arise, but you wouldn't be climbing up the walls at the first setback.

You'd probably attract people into your life who are just like yourself, who are open, generous and relaxed. And the more you were able to give them, the more you would receive. You would tend to help each other and share wealth, and let good things into your life. Just as in the first scenario, acting with an abundance mentality becomes a self-fulfilling prophecy.

So what has all this got to do with asking the Universe for energy? Really, it's just the next step. We've looked at the theory that we attract to us what is most like us, and that the more we give, the more we get. Let's suppose that the Universe works on exactly the same principle. If we are generous, our connection with the universal source of energy will be generous in exactly the same way, except that its resources are *infinite*. All that would remain for us to do is ask for what it is we need.

Here are two methods for asking the universe for energy.

Get yourself comfortable and quiet. Think about what it is you really need. Write it down, with absolute certainty that what you need will be forthcoming, and believe that it will be. Then just let it be, like something nice cooking on a low heat. Don't keep on peeping, just wait until it's ready. It may take a day or a month or a year depending on what you're asking for, but you will get what you need.

This next way immediately attracts a wonderful form of energy. Tell yourself, with absolute certainty and light-heartedness, that something great will happen to you today. Know it with a relaxed, amused delight. As we wrote that and looked out through the window of the study, at the bare trees outside on this mid-march morning, there's a glimpse through the branches of a flawless blue sky, and golden sunlight shows up every detail of the buds that are bursting with life just a few feet away.

This is what happens if you are open to it: you become attuned to the possibility of something great happening to you today. You start to see the things that happen in a new light, wondering if this was what you'd asked for. Maybe *that* was it—just the gift of seeing our own reality directly for a few moments, and being able to recognise all the beauty around us. Or perhaps we will get *even luckier* today! So many things become significant and interesting and magical—and yet it's all just part of your own private game. Nobody has to know. But they will notice something in you has changed.

When you are practised at this, you can often feel as though *everything* that happened to you today was great!

Chapter 36
Everything is by design

Living as though everything is by design is one way to tune into what's really happening in our lives. This is a massively empowering practice, as I'll explain.

First of all though, let's deal with any negative attitudes about this. The idea that everything is by design may seem to encourage fatalism — that we put up with bad things that happen to us because that's just the way things are. Or even worse, that the bad things that happen to us are some form of punishment that we have to just accept.

In fact, that kind of philosophy is the opposite of what our search for energy in this book is all about. *You* are in control — you have the power to make your circumstances and create your reality. Nevertheless, we still insist that everything is by design.

In fact, we *choose* to believe that everything is by design, because it's a belief that gives us great advantages.

Imagine having a mentor or coach in your life who is available at every turn, whether the things that happen to you are good, bad or indifferent. Now this coach — imagine someone who is bubbling with enthusiasm but who is also very intelligent, perceptive, and absolutely dedicated to your success — has a particular style. She believes in the idea that 'action drives out thought' and that you often need to just stop rushing around doing stuff! She thinks that you either get paralysed or over-react in the face of difficulties. She advises you to think things through calmly and with sensitivity to the meaning of this particular moment in your life. So the coach sits us down, makes us comfortable, and asks us some simple questions about the current situation.

This is exactly what it's like to have a belief in the idea that everything is by design. It allows us to look at setbacks as though they were sent as a message. We can make ourselves comfortable, calm down, and see the situation in the context of the bigger picture of our lives. If you know that what has happened to you has a purpose, then you'll be motivated to find out what that purpose is. You will be able to turn any setback into an opportunity for growth, and any doubt about your future into an adventure.

Let me give you an example. In the mid nineties, a friend — let's call him Alan — was offered a chance to move into a new role in the company he worked for. It seemed like an exciting opportunity, with the chance to build a new team, to try out some new ideas, and to really change things for the better. What actually happened was that some people in the organisation seemed to have a vested interest in keeping things exactly as they were. Attempts at change were not only passively resisted, but actively undermined and even sabotaged. The final straw came when senior executives effectively got cold feet about the changes, and decided that ruffling the feathers of people who did not want to change was more trouble than it was worth. Alan was left isolated, powerless, and feeling like he was all dressed up with nowhere to go.

In that kind of situation, there are four things you can do.

You can change the situation. He'd tried that and failed.

You can change yourself. Into someone who accepted that you gave up when the going got tough, just in case you upset a few old boys? He wasn't going to do that.

You can accept the situation. And become bitter and twisted, and dread getting up in the morning to go into a workplace situation that's sucking the energy from you like a sponge? That probably would have been the worst option.

You can walk away. Into the unknown? All the other options were already ruled out — this was all there was left.

Alan left the job and that company, and did so without any knowledge of what he would do next to earn a living, or where the next mortgage payment was coming from.

At that point, there are essentially two views that you can take. Either, you have been the victim of a meaningless set of circumstances which have left you on the canvas. Or you can take the view that what has happened is *by design*.

Alan chose to take the latter view. First he thought about what he had already learned. He realised that when it had come to the crunch, he had some moral fibre to call on, that he was willing to take a risk, and would bet on his own talents to pull him through in some way that the universe hadn't revealed yet. This in itself — taking a risk based on confidence in your own capabilities — is enormously energising. It marks you out, and sets you up to take other big decisions when they are needed.

But Alan was still without a job or even the prospect of one. What was the design in *that*?

Alan reasoned that the design must be a simple one: he had shown some backbone by walking away from an unreasonable situation. The design could only be completed if he then found something that was a reverse image of what he'd walked away from. He was sure that there must be some form of work waiting for him that would maximise his talents, stretch him intellectually, and use his ideas in a creative and powerful way.

Alan responded to an advertisement for a job that seemed very similar to the one he'd walked away from. He then had a remarkable conversation with the recruitment executive, who told him he would be crazy to apply for the job she was advertising, that he was bigger and better than he was allowing himself to be, and that he needed to look for something that was far more interesting and demanding!

Alan only applied for one other post. There was something about the advertisement that caught his eye — a promise of excitement and challenge and novelty. The fact is that the chain of exciting events that ensued is still reverberating in his life today. Alan travelled the world, became successful, had a wonderful time and earned plenty of money. Even more importantly, his belief in his ability to overcome setbacks — that they were just messages sent to guide him — was reinforced, and Alan became someone with supreme self-confidence and quiet personal power.

Let's end on an energising paradox…

Everything in your life has meaning.
But you can take the decision as to what that meaning is.

PART 7

✳

Rock Your World!

The vast possibilities of our great future will become realities only if we make ourselves responsible for that future.

Gifford Pinchod

We're really excited about this part of the book! Now we're getting down to brass tacks and it's time for action!

So far, we've looked at the mind and body as a holistic system, and worked on relaxation, how to tune into the power of the Universe, and to use visualisation to fill our minds and bodies with amazing energy. We've seen how to avoid or defeat energy vampires, attract energy angels, and generate our own energy.

Now you can put all of this into action on a different level. The techniques you've learned so far and the ideas we've been dealing with are all about quick fixes — energy boosts that you can use whenever you need them.

This part of the book though is all about you and how it's possible to examine your past and present to bring energy into your future in a way that is specific to you. It isn't about the you who worries, or is tired, or feels worn down by circumstances. This chapter is about the joyful you, the person who is squeezing every drop of juice from life, who's excited, fired up and ready to act.

You can come back to this section again and again for guidance and inspiration. Use it to remind yourself that the key to being everything you want to be is really very simple.

Think about what you *really* want to be (we have the techniques!).

Visualise what your future will be like (those too!)

Then go out and Rock Your World!

Chapter 37
The future in the past

This section of the book is all about generating the energy you need so that you can create the future that you want, and in this chapter we reveal one way that you can open your mind and heart to what it is that you really want to do.

Are you someone who feels that you haven't yet found your true vocation in life? That you aren't working on something that you are really passionate about, and that you want to change the work you do? Then this chapter is for you.

Even if we only focused on traditional ways of looking at work — that it's something that we do until we are sixty or sixty five, then retire — we'd have to admit that a lifetime of doing work that doesn't satisfy, inspire or play to our sense of fun is a crazy way of going about things. In fact, many people love their jobs so much that the idea of retirement never enters their heads, and it's hard to see where they draw the line of what's work and what isn't.

To be able to choose one's work is a luxury; to be able to earn a living at something that we would do just for the pleasure, interest and fun, without getting paid — well, that is just a far-off dream.

Or is it? Maybe what is needed is the passion and belief to drive us on to connect with what we really want to do, and then keep on pushing until we get what we want. One way we can make that connection is to look into our pasts to remember what it was that we dreamed that we would do when we grew up.

As a child, our friend Kath wanted to be an archaeologist. She was fascinated by discoveries of treasure-filled tombs, and enthralled by stories of Ancient Greek armies marching off to war. There was a fascination with the uniforms of the soldiers, the plumed helmets and the shields and swords.

But Kath did not become an archaeologist and is quite happy not to be one. Though ancient history and pre-history remained an interest, it never developed into a real passion. She suspects now that part of her desire to be an archaeologist was that she was proud of knowing what the word meant!

If you want to reconnect with your dreams of the past, there will probably be several that developed over time, but only some of those would have worked their way into your heart, into the very core of who you are. Unlike Kath, looking back to early childhood might be where you find the seed of what you really want to do. Be open to it. Your first reaction to rediscovering those early passions might be something like "who am I kidding? It's too late now anyway, and I could never really do that — there are too many obstacles in the way".

Don't talk yourself out of things so easily. We recently spoke to someone in their late twenties who had always wanted to be a racing car driver. He considered it to be too late for him now, and was pretty sure that he didn't have enough skill to really make the grade. We asked him if there was anything else about motor-sport that he liked, other than the actual competing. Within five minutes we'd between us come up with a dozen different motor-sport related careers that he would love to be involved in.

To go back to Kath's example, the things that she has now connected with didn't really become passions for her until her early teens. For many people, this can be a really important period to look back on. At that age, you are open to new things and have some reasoning ability. On the other hand, the conventional world of adults hasn't quite got its grips on you. Some teenagers still haven't learned the lesson that they should knuckle down and find the path of least resistance so that they can sleepwalk through the rest of life!

Once you've connected with those old dreams, look at them closely. Imagine what it would be like to earn your living at what you really care about. For Kath, it was ideas, writing, music, photography — any form of artistic beauty and creativity. It doesn't need to be grand, the work just needs to sing to your heart. It might be carpentry or Chartered Accountancy — bridge building or road sweeping. This is not about status — it's about doing your heart's work, the one thing (or two or five things) that will break down the artificial barrier that's been erected between your work and the rest of your life.

We recently had a really difficult 'case' to deal with. A woman called Barbara was planning on a return to paid work with a mixture of fear and dread after a twenty year break during which she brought up her daughters and ran the household. We asked her to look at this as a massive opportunity to do work that would make her want to jump out of bed in the morning. Her reaction was that she had never had a dream of what she really wanted to do. Furthermore, she considered it ridiculous to dream of doing any kind of work that she considered to be 'above her station'. At best she would just get the lowest paid work she could find, because that was all she was capable of doing. What a terribly sad state of affairs! Not because low paid work is necessarily boring and unchallenging, and it's certainly useful to society — but because Barbara really didn't want to do those jobs. But she didn't know what it was that she *did* want to do.

It turned out that during her formative and teenage years, expectations of Barbara were low. In fact, they were non-existent. In her culture, girls were not meant to have careers, and they certainly weren't expected to excel or to enjoy their work. Women were home-makers.

So, what can a person do who really has no dream of work that might be fulfilling?

Well, there are two options. The first is, forget it. Accept your lot in life, but on no account moan about it. That's how Energy Vampires are born. Do what your parents and peers always expected you to do, knuckle down and get on with it. There are other ways to be happy, and that is fine. But realise now that if you *don't* find other ways to be happy you will always have a sense of what might have been — if only you had taken a more powerful decision, if you had only learned more and done more, if only you had the courage to really push yourself beyond the expectations of others.

The other option for someone who cannot dream of doing fulfilling work, and who cannot imagine what kind of work that might be, is to stop kidding yourself. I don't believe that you lack imagination. In your secret moments, I am sure, you allow yourself a fraction of a second to see a new you, learning exciting new skills and ways to live, talking with interesting people, being inwardly satisfied with your achievements. Indulge in that imagined scene right now! What you have is not a lack of imagination, but a fear of standing out in the crowd, of offending society by rising to take your rightful place.

Create the future you want!

Chapter 38
Energy and the path to your dreams

A basic but important question we have to ask ourselves about personal energy is, what are we going to do with it all? How can we direct it, use it wisely and effectively?

When done well, setting goals for yourself can help you to use energy effectively. In addition, the practice of setting goals can be energising in itself, as long as it doesn't turn into yet another list-of-things-to-do exercise that makes you feel defeated and incompetent by the end of the day.

It's great to be clear about what you want to achieve. The trick is to get that clarity in a way that supports and inspires you, and makes you feel great about yourself.

So let's take a different approach. Imagine that you had absolute clarity about what you want to achieve with the rest of your life, and the values that you will live by. Each day would then be an energising way of putting those values into practice and moving towards what you want to achieve.

Let's take it one step further. If the values you want to live the rest of your life by are so powerful, strong, inspirational and in tune with your spiritual, ethical and intellectual needs, then it's the *process* of living that becomes important — an end in itself. Your 'personal objectives' then become a by-product of a deeply satisfying way of living your life.

When most people set their objectives, they are concentrating on two kinds of things. The first is what they can *do* — work harder, manage time better, learn a new skill, etc. The second is what they can *get* — a faster car, a bigger house, a more attractive lover.

We're suggesting that you focus on what you can *be*.

Let me try to make this clearer by using an example. Many of the great European cathedrals of the middle ages were built over the span of many lifetimes. Imagine a devout stonemason, a master craftsman who is absolutely certain that the efforts of his mind and hands are to the greater glory of God. He is building something that will not be finished in his lifetime — the major 'objective', the completed cathedral, is beyond his reach, and he will never see the finished whole, of which his efforts are just a part. But the stonemason has values. Those values are to do with dedicating his work to some higher meaning, creating beauty, and devoting all his skills and talents to the task in hand. He does not judge his work or his life by how the 'building project' is progressing: he judges it by the quality of his contribution, and whether or not he is giving the best of himself.

We're not advocating that anyone toil away in obscurity (though many great people have). Nor are we saying that one should find refuge in the certainties of organised religion (though many people do). What we are saying is that when we live by our values, when we can be proud of our work, when we aim to improve everything that we touch or think about or do, we can live life with the massive energy that comes from being true to ourselves.

It's a curious fact that we sometimes have to remind ourselves of our values. After all, you'd think that what we have in our hearts is always accessible to us. But it takes practice and a strong character to keep our values at the forefront of what we do, and the ability to set a new course when we're battered by the storms of life. The way to do this is simply to ask ourselves the right questions.

We've already looked at one very empowering question — *what would you do if you knew you could not fail?* In a later chapter we'll also ask ourselves about the power of imagined hindsight in the chapter called 'Deathbed Scene". But for now, here are some other powerful, energising questions:

When I am at my very best, who am I?

When I am the person I want to be, what do I do?

What do I look like, what do I see, hear and feel?

Three questions, then. The first two focus on what we already know. They are the questions that help us establish our values. Perhaps when *you* are the best that you can be you're courageous, forthright, confident, single minded, truthful. Think about this and make your own list of qualities. My list may not mean much to you, but it's absolutely inspiring to me! So don't let your list of qualities be about what you *should* be like, but about what you really feel is at the heart of who you are.

Once you have that list, imagine living every single day by those values, ensuring that your personal qualities are the ones you keep to. It's simple, powerful and energising!

The third question is of a different kind. *When you are at your best, what do you look like, what do you see, hear and feel?*

The answer to this question will keep you on track for living your values. When you use your imagination to see, hear and touch your surroundings as you want them to be, when you imagine living life in harmony with your innermost values, you are telling your sub-conscious mind to allow you to create the conditions for making these dreams come true. So get comfortable, close your eyes, use your breath to focus and quieten the mind. Visualise yourself at your best, living your values every day. Then go out into the world and be the person you imagine you can be.

Chapter **39**

Take action!

> *There are costs and risks to a program of action, but they are far less than the long range risks and costs of comfortable inaction.*
> JOHN F KENNEDY

As JFK suggested, there are a thousand different reasons not to act. Let's look at some of them so that we can be realistic about this. Then we'll look at a few reasons why taking action is an energising and satisfying way to live.

Sometimes we don't act because we are scared. Imagine telling someone how attractive you find them, only to be rejected, possibly in public. Or you may write down your thoughts for public appraisal, as we are doing now, only to find them belittled and disparaged. On the other hand, we may never have these words published, and this failure would mean that we had wasted an enormous amount of time and effort.

You might gamble on changing your career, only to find that your new path is disastrous, and leaves you wondering where the next mortgage payment is coming from.

Three kinds of things, then, keep us from acting: fear of rejection, fear of failure, and the perception of danger (which is essentially the same thing).

It's true to say that fear can serve us well: it helps to keep us from doing foolhardy and dangerous things. But very often, these fears are simply the result of the lack of confidence that was somehow built into us when we were children. That, and the curious fact that we seem to live as though we are going to go on forever, that we have all the time in the world (see chapter 42), and that we can always do something of real significance some time later.

What would your life be like if you did the things you really want to do, and said the things you really want to say? Yes, you'd be risking rejection and failure, but without at least a spark of danger, you risk being timid, achieving little, and growing old with too many regrets. As someone once said—life is not a rehearsal... you aren't going to get another chance to run through it all again, with a little more action and courage next time. There's only *this* time. There is only now.

There is a special rule related to action. In every situation that calls for action, have the outcome you want to achieve firmly in mind. Know what it is you want, and devise a strategy to get it.

This can sound manipulative, but if you are coming from a manipulative frame of mind, people will sense that in you and your 'strategy' will come to nothing. So don't worry that this is going to transform you into a wicked Svengali figure—it won't. What it does is simply give you a tool to help you achieve what you want, rather than allowing yourself to be a victim of circumstance, or someone who is blown in new directions like a leaf in the wind.

Let's suppose you are standing in line at the supermarket checkout. You see that the woman on the checkout is bored, grumpy and uncommunicative. Her mood seems to worsen with each customer. You decide that somehow, you will make this person's day a little brighter for a few seconds, without patronising, irritating or embarrassing her. You set yourself that challenge.

How do you do it?

Well, that's your challenge, not mine!

Can you see what this will do for your energy levels? And can you see what it could do for your own self-esteem and success if you decide, before you embark on a course of action, on what your outcome will be? This is what Stephen R Covey, in his book 'The Seven Habits of Highly Effective People", calls 'beginning with the end in mind'. Use it before you go into a difficult meeting; maybe you want to 'win', or perhaps the best outcome would be to find a constructive way forward. Before you walk in your house after a hard day's work, do you want to transmit all the anxieties and problems of the day to your spouse? Or do you want an evening of harmony and peace? If the latter, make that your objective and bring it about.

Is there such a thing as a situation in which I don't want a specific outcome? And doesn't this way of being encourage an uptight, stressed out view of life where you always have to be achieving something or other?

Well, it isn't necessarily about 'achievement'. Suppose all you want to do is relax — in fact, you want to doze for a while. You can't get much less 'driven' than that! But if your spouse or kids burst into the room while you're napping, wake you up, and you then proceed to spend the next couple of hours griping about never being able to get any rest, then the situation has clearly developed into something that benefits no one. What you could have done was clearly formulated an outcome (dozing), and told the family that you would have a nap for thirty minutes (the action that guarantees your outcome).

There is no harm in knowing what you want. It's how you go about getting it that determines your strength of character and shows your values in action.

Chapter 40
Fake it!

There are two amazing qualities of the human mind. The first is the mind's ability to change itself and the reality of the environment it's in. That's what most of this book is about — making a powerful connection between the power of the mind, body and spirit in a way that gives us access to huge reservoirs of energy so that you can overcome difficulties, realise your dreams and live life to the full.

The other intriguing quality of the mind is that it often seems like an iceberg — that is, only one tenth of it is on show, and the rest lies submerged, hard or impossible to know in its entirety. But it's the 90% below the surface that determines much of our behaviour, our goals and our achievements — in fact, the very way that we live.

There are many beautiful theories about the submerged or hidden part of the mind — the sub-conscious — and we want to share one here that we ask you to open up your *conscious* mind to consider. What we're about to consider is capable of changing the way you think about your life, and of giving you a great sense of self-revelation.

Suppose for a moment that every single action you take, every way of perceiving and thinking about the world is designed to bring about an objective.

Now, imagine that the objective that your behaviour is trying to bring about is one that is hidden to your conscious mind. In other words, consider the possibility that *everything that you do is designed to meet an objective that you consciously don't want and haven't approved of.*

How could such a state of affairs come about? Well, the theory is that in early childhood we process huge amounts of information that are absolutely new. We have no experience against which to judge the inputs of our senses. We must creatively interpret everything in a way that makes sense for us and allows each individual to deal with the world in a way that is safe, and has internal cohesion.

It may be, for instance, that the world of adults and siblings in early childhood taught us to be **seen and not heard**, and that there were severe punishments for not sticking to that rule. We internalise the lesson at a very deep level of the subconscious in such a way that it becomes ingrained in us and we develop a lifestyle that is absolutely dedicated to achieving the objectives that our early experiences taught us were the right way to live with others. Everything we do (using this example) strives towards the achievement of being obscure and unnoticed.

As we mature we may develop other conscious objectives such as wanting to communicate assertively. But — the theory goes — the conscious objective is practically worthless and impossible to achieve if we aren't able to overcome the early conditioning that taught us to be timid, quiet, and unobtrusive.

If any of the above resonated with you, you may have had an *aha!* moment where you realised what has been holding you back for all these years. For others, it will take many more years to come to this self-realisation. And still others will already have transcended this part of their conditioning (though we advise you to be careful of assuming that is true).

So, how can you overcome negative early programming that is sabotaging the wishes of your conscious mind at every turn? In fact, almost every section of this book has techniques on how to do exactly that, but the one we're now going to discuss is all about *faking it*.

What we mean by *faking* is the openness to experiment with the possibility of what you could be if your conscious and subconscious minds were in absolute agreement.

What would it be like if today you were to go through the world as though you were already the person you wanted to be? Most likely, this will mean that you are going to have to override the self-limiting beliefs programmed into your young sub-conscious. This can be threatening to parts of your personality. One way to do it — and you may notice that we recommend this attitude a lot! — is to pretend, just for now that it's just a game.

So let's have some harmless fun.

Act as if you already have everything you need. Walk through the world as though you own it, as if it were in your power to dissolve, with a sweep of the hand, everything that was previously holding you back.

If before you were shy, *act as if* **you are now a confident, sociable and likeable *superstar*.** Imagine it, see it in your mind's eye, then do it.

If before you felt that you often spoke too much, and unwisely, *act as if* **you are now a wise, compassionate and thoughtful sage.** Imagine how you would sound, and how you would feel. Then go out and do it.

If before you were fearful, *act as if* **you are now courageous, fearless and brave.** Picture the scene in all its detail — then just go and act it out.

Unlike other animals, we can use our imaginations to overcome our programmed responses to the world. When you reinvent yourself, you can reinvent the world. Act as if you can today, then *stay in character.*

Chapter 41
Set yourself a challenge

This chapter is about challenging your mind and spirit in a way that generates personal energy. Just as a body builder uses resistance training to build muscle, we can gradually set ourselves more difficult and interesting challenges to the habitual way that we do things. Like weight lifters, though, it isn't just the resistance training that guarantees growth—it's also about nutrition, relaxation and rest. Use the other chapters in this book to give yourself the right nutrition and rest for the mind through visualisation, mindful breathing, and all the other techniques we've been discussing.

There's a good reason for challenging ourselves on a daily basis. The fact is, it's exhilarating, satisfying and meaningful. Just like someone training at the gym for the sake of the rush of endorphins produced by physical exercise, we can challenge ourselves just for the hell of it. It's a way of waking up, of refusing to accept a life of sleepwalking, and of filling ourselves with energy.

So, what's the holistic version of the weight lifters challenge? Let's try this—imagine carrying out an activity—let's call it **X**—in the following way:

You are absolutely committed to **X**. You will complete it without distraction. There is nothing you would rather be doing.

You will bring all your skills, experience and training to bear on the completion of **X**.

You are determined to carry out **X** with style, grace, and flair. You are confident that the results you obtain will stand up to the best that anyone doing a similar activity anywhere in the world could do. You are at the top of your game when it comes to **X**, and you know with certainty that there are very few people who can touch you.

Think about how that feels, exactly what it would be like.

Now imagine how you would feel if activity **X** is *tying your shoelaces*.

When you imagined activity **X** as something that was challenging, complex, in some way grand, you probably imagined yourself to be totally absorbed in the task, filled with energy and enthusiasm for it. Now that you realise that the activity is a simple, commonplace daily task for millions of people, perhaps you don't feel quite so proud of yourself.

You simply won't get feelings of satisfaction and energy from doing simple things that are not challenging, even if you do them to the very best of your ability. It isn't just the sense of accomplishment that is missing. It's the enjoyment of the moment, the loss of self-consciousness and timelessness that we can achieve when we are operating at our best in a challenging environment.

Let's talk about a physical example again, just because we know of a recent real-life experience that illustrates how the mind relates to the challenges it's set.

Amy was trying to increase her running times, and had got stuck. She'd worked her way gradually from an average speed of 8kph to 9kph. But for all her efforts, she could not run even a tiny bit faster than that. The more she aimed to run at 9.1kph, the more exhausted Amy became. This went on for weeks without success, and the longer it went on, the more Amy became convinced that she just wasn't built to run any faster.

Amy put her mind to work on this problem, and decided that the thing to do was drop her speed back down to about 8.5kph, then gradually build her way back up again. The logic was that she might somehow build new reservoirs of energy that would push her through the old barrier. She also wanted to get her mind back into habits of success, instead of failure. This is often a great way of handling our personal objectives. Many people tend to aim too high, and then beat themselves up when they fail. So a realistic but challenging target can help build our self-confidence. She dropped her objective back down to 8.5kph.

It turned out to be a disaster. Now Amy was struggling just to make 8.5, and on a really good day could perhaps run at 8.7kph. This was depressing. Her mind was working overtime on excuses (you've been working too hard recently and it's showing up in your body), rationalisations (it's purely temporary and you'll get back to your old times soon) and self-justifications (you're getting older, what do you expect?).

This last one (I'm getting older) was a marvellous way of allowing herself to give up. We shouldn't always dismiss 'giving up' as an act of cowardice or failure of will if in fact there are other more useful ways of spending our time. But Amy's sub-conscious continued to scream "Failure! Too old!", and she deliberately put herself in a Churchillian frame of mind: *never* give in.

What happened next was a surprise. Amy realised that she had to come up with something new. All the old ways of challenging her personal-best running time had ended in failure. Just trying harder was having the opposite of the desired effect: the attempt to break through 9.0kph had resulted in running slower. Then it came to her. Instead of trying to run at 9.1kph, she would run at 10.1 kph.

The results were astonishing. That day, Amy ran at an average speed of 9.5 kph. She *smashed* through the 9.0 barrier.

So what was going on there? Amy's body hadn't changed. Her running shoes were the same, and her technique was no different.

By aiming for something 'impossibly' out of reach, Amy had sent a message to her subconscious mind that there was a new target. She did this in a relaxed way, but with a sense of excitement. She somehow knew in her bones before she started the run that she would make a breakthrough.

To sum it all up, Amy had changed her reality by changing the way that she thought about things, and the tool she used to do that was to set herself a massive challenge. She had aimed for the stars, and hit the moon.

Chapter 42
Deathbed scene

> *May you live all the days of your life*
> JONATHAN SWIFT

Some readers may find this exercise a bit morbid. Others will find it incredibly powerful. Done in the right way, thinking about your own mortality can be very energising.

Cast your mind forward to the end of your long, long life. You are waiting calmly for death, thinking back on everything you did. You see clearly what you might have done differently, opportunities that passed you by, and where you took the right decisions and experienced marvellous, fulfilling phases of your life.

This exercise can give you a powerful perspective on your life so far, and what you will do with the rest of it. It will give you the energy to use the rest of your life to do the things that make a real difference to you. You'll get a clear sense of your real mission, and the energy to carry it through: but beware, when played with a serious intent, this is a dangerous game. Prepare to face your own truth!

Are you spending time in your life on things that don't really serve you, that you excuse as a way of 'relaxing'? We can all let our guards done some time – and so we should. It's great to have a good time. But is watching TV, for example, really that much fun? Is accepting the low-grade, lowest-common-denominator view of culture pushed at us by the media really an innocent way of winding down? Or is it draining you of the life blood you could be using to fulfil ourselves in fantastic, imaginative ways?

You decide!

So there you are, on your deathbed, looking back to this day, today. There's a decision in front of you. Something that will send you on a path that will shape your destiny. Perhaps one path is well trodden—a little boring perhaps, but familiar and safe. The other is overgrown and unfamiliar—but perhaps holds out the promise of excitement and passion. Do you take the path less travelled, or the one that promises an easy passage? Look back to your decision from your death-bed. What was the right thing to do?

Now, imagine that you just have time to ask yourself some questions. Look back over your time on earth and decide—

Which were the most important things that you did? Did they make you famous, or were they quiet acts of unnoticed heroism? Were they acts of leadership, or refusals to conform to what was expected of you? Did you bring truth and beauty into the world, or low-grade junk for recycling? You can look back on it all now. And you can make the right decisions, today.

As an old person waiting for an end to your time on earth, do you look back with regret or profound happiness? Ask yourself—what was I at my best? Not, what did I achieve? But: what was I?

Were you fearless and calm in the face of provocation, or did you walk the other way? Are you loyal to friends, or have they long since left you to die alone? Did you take a chance and give and receive as much love as you could, or did you bottle it all up inside, waiting for the perfect opportunity?

And now the final question: what will they inscribe on your tombstone? What will be the few words that will summarise you, your life and your character?

The idea of all this is to bring the answers back into the present. The responses we give to these questions are the secret ambitions of our hearts, the keys to life as we would like to live it. The way you live depends on your energetic actions, and your actions depend on your thoughts. Take your death-bed thoughts, pump them full of life and energy, then go out and live the future you imagine.

Chapter 43
Energy in action –
more healthy basics

Throughout this book we've emphasised that the mind and body are part of a single system. As you start to think about the amazing future you can now create for yourself, let's think once again about how to get and live in the healthiest possible body — one that will whisk you through your new energetic adventures.

Of course, as you'd expect there's visualisation involved! You can do this simple technique first, before starting on a new way of eating or exercising, and then repeat often. Read through first, then go back and do each step.

Technique!

Maximum Health and Energy

First, find somewhere quiet where you will not be disturbed. Close your eyes, follow the breath and quieten the mind.

Bring to mind a picture of yourself as you would be if you were at your absolute healthiest and most energetic. This is the you that is going to emerge after eating and drinking healthily, exercising regularly, and resting deeply. It's the you who has been kissed by the sun, and who knows how to minimise stress and maximise energy.

> See how you move; watch how you smile and interact with others; hear what they say about your new appearance and attitude. Get the picture just right–change the size, saturate the colours, make the sounds pleasing, smooth and at just the right pitch that is right for you. This is the dynamic new you, after you've given yourself the holistic Energy! Treatment.
>
> Quietly tell your sub-conscious mind that this is the new version of yourself that you wish to create.

You have now set your mind up for success in becoming the healthiest, most energetic person you can be. Your sub-conscious will work on your behalf to bring your desired self into reality. The sub-conscious mind is your servant, and you've just given it very clear instructions! Let's take a look now at the details of how you can treat your body, to help the mind to bring about the new, healthier, more energetic you.

Have you considered why it is that so many new diet plans come and go—why so many people are willing to give over their money time and time again to try some new fad? Why don't the diets work? Yes, I know we've all seen the pictures of 'miracle' dieters, but if they were the norm, the diet industry would be a fraction of the size it is now.

There are a few facts that explain why *diets don't work*. The first is that most diet plans concentrate only on the body—they don't treat the whole person, body, mind and spirit. Secondly, they concentrate on weight, when they should be concentrating on energy and well-being. Next, they haven't got beyond the one-size-fits-all approach, which doesn't recognise that we all have different needs, attitudes, metabolisms, desired outcomes, and amounts of spare time.

Every month, 'scientific research' seems to come up with new conclusions which contradict the previous month's announcements. Is red wine a terrible poison or the best guard against heart disease there's ever been? Could it be that this inconsistency is partly due to the fact that we are all different, and that we can start to use our intuition, good sense, and careful experimentation to find what works for us?

The rest of this chapter looks at some of the most important aspects of holistic health, and points out some of the main competing theories on what works and what doesn't. The main thing is to experiment and find what works for you. The obvious answers are already known to you—regarding smoking, for instance—but you'll also find that your body has deeper, more subtle wisdom about what it *needs*, which isn't always the same thing as what the conscious mind tells you that you *want*. Play with it. Trust yourself.

Hydration

There are two main schools of thought regarding hydration (drinking sufficient amounts of water). They could hardly disagree more about the 'correct' advice to give. Let's look at the increasingly dominant argument first...

Water is the key to good health and vitality. You should drink at least 2.5 litres a day, and make sure that you never get dehydrated. This will help you detoxify your body (i.e. flush out the toxins that accumulate in the blood-stream and the organs), which will ensure that the body's energy won't be drained by the constant effort to wash away poisons. Drinking copious amounts of water is also good for your skin, hair, and just about every other aspect of good health and appearance that you can think of. As an added bonus, drinking lots of water will give you a feeling of fullness, and therefore help you to eat less and lose weight.

There are also strong opponents of this view. They are not just neutral about the benefits of drinking lots of water, they are downright against it. The anti-water lobby also has convincing arguments: digestion is a crucial part of the body's functioning, and depends upon the right chemicals in the stomach to ensure efficient break down of foods. Water drunk at meal times is especially damaging, as it dilutes the digestive juices and slows the passage of food through the body, causing the build-up of toxic waste in the gut. The anti-water lobby also believes that drinking so much water is essentially 'unnatural': if we all ate more unprocessed, water rich food, there would be no need to supplement our water intake at all.

So where does the truth lie? Well, it lies in *your* body. Most of the healthy people I know judiciously mix both approaches. They drink lots of fresh water, but they don't do so at meal times. And they also agree that less water would be required if our diets were 'perfect'. If we drank less diuretic liquids such as tea and coffee, and ate less foods which lacked the water and nutrients that are in fruit and vegetables, then we wouldn't need so much water! Find the balance that is right for you.

Nutritional Supplements

These days we need nutritional supplements because modern farming methods remove so much of the goodness from our foods. It is more difficult than ever to get a balanced diet, which is the reason why there are so many allergies and similar medical conditions such as asthma and eczema that used to be more rare. We have to make sure that we get a good balance of vitamins and minerals.

The other side of the argument goes like this. Actually, it's easier than ever to get a balanced diet with foods rich in vitamins and minerals. The organic farming movement is growing and the difference in price between organic and non-organic foods is narrowing. The vitamins and minerals found in supplements are also in a form that is extremely difficult to digest, and the added effort that the body needs to make to process them can put strain on internal organs and actually make us more tired. The answer is to eat a wide variety of unprocessed natural foods that contain the nutrients in a form that we can digest easily.

This is another area where many experts actually take from the best of each approach, suggesting that supplements are sometimes needed to combat specific conditions, such as rheumatism, that normal prescription medicines fail to deal with.

Again, the choice is yours. Be aware that there are increasingly more 'natural' supplements becoming available, and if you can afford them, give them a go. Use supplements that are as 'organic' as possible — derived from food, rather than chemically synthesised. For an energy boost, some people find that spirulina and wheatgrass powders mixed with water are excellent. By all means try them, but not as a substitute for healthy, balanced eating.

Food

The two extreme views on food that I see most often are easy to choose between. On the one hand, there is 'food' as it exists for the Dieting Industry. Essentially, food is something you fight — if you're not careful, it will make you overweight, and that will start to erode your self-image and confidence. One problem with that approach is that if you fail to lose weight even though you are trying your *hardest* to diet, well then why not fall off the wagon completely and just sit and eat fast foods, chocolates and pizzas?

Perhaps the diet industry has peaked, and soon people will realise that the cycles of weight loss, weight gain, self-denial, guilt and bingeing are built into the dieting way of life. Essentially, the whole idea is a destructive one.

On the other hand, a shift of consciousness happens when we realise that we eat not only for pleasure, but for energy and health. Burn your tape measures! Melt down your bathroom scales! Eat food that makes you feel good, not just today, but tomorrow. Eat wholesome, unprocessed, natural foods that haven't been dosed with chemicals, salt and animal fats. See and feel yourself growing stronger, shining with good health, and brimming with self confidence.

Chapter **44**

A tool for your success

Success in any endeavour not only *needs* energy, it also *generates* energy. For that reason, we're going to give you an excellent tool that when used regularly, kept sharp, and applied with skill, will bring you massive, satisfying success.

The process includes the seven elements which are all you need to be successful. They are deceptively simple on their own, but when combined into a system they are amazingly powerful.

The seven components of the process are:

Attention
Concentration
Energy
Health
Intelligence
Gumption
Holistic Attitude

And if you haven't realised yet, this is the Ace-High process! Let's look at each of these in turn...

Attention: Whatever we give attention to, we attract into our lives. If you concentrate on health, that's what you'll attract. If you concentrate on ill-health, you'll get that instead. It's the same with success and failure, love and hate, energy and exhaustion. Put your attention on the things you want in your life. Visualise them powerfully using the techniques you have learned in this book.

On a daily basis, put your attention on the goals that you want to achieve. A simple statement, and a simple-sounding piece of advice, but it's amazing how often it's neglected. If you don't give attention to your objectives, you will not condition your mind to achieve them. Attention to a subject generates ideas. Ideas bring about action. Action brings the conditions that you require. There is a direct link between your attention and your results.

Concentration: This is not the same thing as attention. Attention is the process of deciding what you will bring your concentration to. Concentration is the hard work of being focused on what needs to be done. Its brother is will power, and its cousin is gumption. It isn't easy to concentrate—especially in the industrialised, Internetted world where there are constant competing claims for our time and our energy.

Without concentration—the determined, wilful exercise of our capacity to think and work hard on the matter in hand—there can be no real success or achievement. You don't hear that too many times in self-help books, because it's uncomfortable for people. Hard work? That's boring, puritanical, not-fun. It's also the truth.

Energy: Paying attention and applying concentration are essentially tasks for the mind. The frequent practice of mindful attention will make you sensitive to the opportunities around you. Wilful concentration will focus the ideas you need to apply to those opportunities. But without energy, you will be unable to bring the fruits of your attention and concentration into existence. There are at least fifty-two ways to cultivate and multiply your personal energy—and they are all in this book!

Health: At least part of the energy you generate is physical, and therefore depends on your health. But as we've seen, personal health is about the relationship between the mind, body and spirit. Use the mind to visualise your body's health, and use the spirit to guide the values you set your body to work on. Look after all three and you set up a virtuous circle of wellbeing.

Intelligence: The exercise of intelligence is absolutely essential to bring your ideas and plans into being. There are different kinds of intelligence, of course, and developing and using each one of them will not only underpin your success—it is a magnificent undertaking in its own right.

I like Howard Gardner's categories of intelligence. Be aware that all of them are in some way crucial to you — either in furthering your aims or for their own sake, to make your time on earth that much more interesting and enjoyable. Here are Gardner's seven categories of intelligence:

1. Linguistic (as in a poet)
2. Logical–mathematical (as in a scientist)
3. Musical (as in a composer)
4. Spatial (as in a sculptor or airline pilot)
5. Bodily kinesthetic (as in an athlete or dancer)
6. Interpersonal (as in a salesman or teacher)
7. Intrapersonal (exhibited by individuals with accurate views of themselves)

Gumption: We've already spoken about this — it's what keeps you going when your ideas and actions run into trouble. It's the Churchillian spirit, the never-say-die quality that is an essential part of any really worthwhile success.

Holistic Attitude: So far, you've paid attention to what you really want from life, and concentrated on what you need to do to make sure your ideas are sound. You've invested your ideas with energy and action, worked on your good health to make sure your energy doesn't run out, and used the scalpel of your intelligence like a surgeon, to make fine distinctions about the nature of everything that you do.

Running like a thread through all of this is the holistic attitude. This is the frame of mind that brings all the other elements together, ensuring that your efforts are not only successful, but also worthwhile.

What profiteth a man if he gain the whole world, but lose his soul?

This is a question that comes from the holistic, spiritual sides of our natures, the part of us that wants to align our objectives with our values, and wants to give as much as it gets. The holistic attitude goes beyond personal gain, and looks for the gain of all; it is the part of us that goes even further, that sees the world and everything in it as part of a system of which we are crucial parts, a system that's affected by our actions.

Chapter 45
Everyday heroism

We all have our heroes, some of whom are famous and known to many people. These are the humans who have done great deeds, faced trials and tribulations with courage, and changed the world for the better in some way. Perhaps you think of T.E. Lawrence (Lawrence of Arabia) at one end of the spectrum, or Mother Teresa at the other. Perhaps you think of great artists and other creative people who brought new ideas and beauty into the world while all around laughed at or rejected them.

Then there are the closer-to-home heroes, who patiently cope with setbacks that would crush weaker spirits, who rise above their circumstances, and become quiet examples of how to go about living. Very few ever hear their names, and such heroes go about their business unrecognised.

Both kinds of hero are generators of energy. We look at their lives and feel motivated to be like them, to show the same degree of courage, intelligence, determination or enthusiasm. Their achievements can goad us into action, or steer us into wisdom. They make us feel that life is short and that there is still much to do.

So the question is, do such people have anything in common? Or are there as many kinds of heroism as there are heroes? Is there some nugget of truth that we can take away, to use when we require heroic actions from ourselves? Or is heroism actually a way of life, a way of looking at the world?

The common denominator of both kinds of heroism does in fact come down to how we view the world. It is a frame of mind, and although it may result in one decisive moment of action that brings fame and fortune, heroism grows in a soil we can do much to cultivate. The common denominator among heroes is that their actions are designed to bring about some objective, and their objectives spring directly from their values.

The key then is to know exactly what your values are. Or rather, be aware of them as they emerge and are shaped by your experience. Values can and do change over time and that is a natural and organic process — as long as they do not change for the sake of convenience or with an eye for the main chance. Some of us value truth, beauty, or freedom and dedicate ourselves to art, science or the spiritual life; others value the human spirit itself, and dedicate themselves to the wellbeing of others. No one can teach you what your values are, although much educational effort is dedicated to steering us towards socially acceptable values. But only you know what is in your heart.

The point is that someone who is grounded in their values is able to act from them. This brings about a certain consistency of behaviour and attitude. We sense when people are true to themselves. We find it admirable and recognise that this internal harmony is the stuff of which heroism is made. This is why heroic deeds have come to be associated with a particular kind of personality — the hero is the person who is most true to himself.

There are other advantages of acting from our values. After all, we may never be put to the test in a way that reveals our 'heroism' in the action-hero sense. It may be that that isn't part of the make-up of our personalities. The first advantage of having clear values and acting in accordance with them is that we develop unshakeable self-confidence. No one can stop actions that come from the heart.

Besides self-confidence, the person who acts from their values develops tremendous charisma. To be 'sorted', to be a person who knows what she believes in and is prepared to back up her beliefs with action, is to be extremely attractive to others. Charisma doesn't necessarily mean to have a 'big' personality, to be larger than life. True charisma is a quality that's recognised by the discerning.

You can see then, why we believe that living in accordance with our values is essential for boosting personal energy over the long term. It develops self-confidence, bestows charisma, and gives us the chance to be everyday heroes.

Chapter 46
Suspend your disbelief

Throughout this book we've occasionally encouraged you to suspend your disbelief. Now we want to explore this idea a little more, because we believe that it is a key to boosting your energy, your opportunities and your sheer joie de vivre.

Suspending disbelief allows you to consider things that once seemed outlandish and strange, and you can experiment with them. This is exciting, motivating and fun.

Of course, we don't just accept anything that comes our way, and adopt it with total belief. That would be gullible. What we do is open ourselves to new and sometimes strange possibilities. Someone once said that new ideas are first laughed at, then feared, before they become the new orthodoxy. Being open to new ideas will mark you out from the crowd.

Suspending your disbelief allows your imagination to run wild. It gives you permission to lose yourself in new experiences and ideas. If you don't do that, you will never be able to enjoy strange sounding new conceptions, or judge them intelligently. As an example, imagine that you were a film critic. You see the film which is a romantic comedy, but your review consists of your amazement that anyone could be taken in by two-dimensional pictures projected onto a large screen, and react to them as though they were real.

What you do when you go to the cinema or read a work of fiction is *suspend your disbelief*. You don't feel that there's anything dangerous about it — you know that it's part of the experience of enjoying art. However, some adults would find it difficult to admit that they really enjoyed a film for small children. Children suspend their disbelief much more easily — they have a less jaundiced experience of the world by which to judge. But an adult might feel embarrassed to become emotionally involved with something 'childish' that is obviously fiction.

This feeling of being caught out by investing our emotions in something that turns out to not be true is one of the things that stops us from being open to new ideas. After all, new ways of doing things are meant to be the truth — how embarrassing if we signed up to some unbelievable nonsense that was later found to be a con.

It's with these attitudes that we can accidentally cut ourselves off from large parts of experience. A refusal to open to new ideas is a notorious sign of ageing. Novelty is sometimes difficult and challenging — far better to stay with what you know — or so it seems.

All of this doesn't mean that we are going to suddenly ask you to believe in UFOs and Alien Abductions. Although, it has to be said, that we find those less ridiculous than the idea that human beings are the only intelligent life forms in a universe which is vast beyond our comprehension. Given the huge numbers of solar systems and planets, that seems an unlikely idea, doesn't it? It's based on having a closed mind that holds that the human species is the only one with a moral sense and the ability to reason, when the chances of life supporting environments arising in other parts of the cosmos is quite high. Anyway, that is just an example, but do let us know if you have absolute proof of Aliens!

It takes courage to be open to new ideas, and it takes a sense of fun. These are the very things that add spice to life. And what if — what a powerful question that is! — what if you were to stumble on something that really helped you? When you come across a big idea, roll it around in your mouth. Savour it. If it feels like there is fun to be had, or some truth to be understood, temporarily suspend your disbelief and act as though it's true.

What kind of idea, perhaps you are asking?

Well, what if the whole of the Universe came into being because of a conscious thought? In other words, that instead of a God (or maybe because of one) there is a Universal Mind. Without thoughts arising in that Universal mind, nothing else arises. Everything we see around us is an effect of the thinking of the Universal Mind. Or, what if mind is static energy and thought is the dynamic version of it, so that everything we sense about us is just a thought in the Universal Mind? Ok, if you've come this far, then what if our own minds, which use our individual brains to think, are just a part of the bigger Mind that has brought everything else into existence?

If that were true, your own mind would have the properties of the Universal Mind of which it's a part — in other words, you too can create things in the real world through the power of your thoughts.

Many of you will know that these ideas have been around for quite a long time. In the twenties they were written about by Charles Haanel (in 'The Master Key'), who spread the word that all human achievement depends upon our connection with the forces that brought us into being. My response when I first came across it wasn't to set up intellectual arguments for and against — it was to act as though this idea is correct.

Try over a long period to bring things into your life that are good for you and for the Universe as a whole. Try manifesting physical and mental energy, for instance, just by thinking about it. If you've been doing the exercises in this book, you already know how to do that. You can even try to manifest wealth, and you might just be amazed at the results.

Chapter 47
The power of creativity

Some people are scared of 'creativity'. It's often thought of as something that 'other people' do—those who have the luxury of being impractical. Some of us carry around stereotypes about creativity, and dismiss 'touchy-feely' activities as the antithesis of what real life is like.

At the other end of the spectrum, artists for the last century or more have been put on a pedestal and worshipped as creative geniuses. The act of creativity is seen as being exceptional. The assumption is that creativity cannot be taught or learned—you are either born with it or you aren't.

Creativity can be exceptional and it can produce exceptional results. But it *can* also be learned, put to great use on everyday practical problems, and it is arguably the one thing that will make the biggest difference to your success and even your happiness.

So what is creativity, what are its personal and overall benefits, and how can we use it?

Creativity is a process that always starts with thought—an idea, a conception, a sense of something. The thought can be encapsulated in words, or it can be an image, a remembered or experienced sound that takes our attention, or even a texture. All of these kinds of thoughts are responses to the environment, or memories of past experiences, or a combination of both. This is an important point, because if creativity is sparked by combinations of inputs, we can deliberately stimulate the environment or our minds to start the process.

There are huge benefits to creativity. Everything around us that has been brought into being by humanity is a result of the process. Before there were bridges, there were thoughts of bridges. There were problems to be solved (how do we cross a river quickly and easily?) and experiences to be drawn on (use of wood laid across streams, natural bridges formed by nature) that were combined into a solution. Then the solutions were refined, improved upon, even made majestic.

In the medium and long terms, if you are creative, if you use your thoughts to bring new things or ideas into the world, you'll mark yourself out as someone with exceptional talents. Creative people do not accept things as they are — they improve, refine, amend, enhance and build upon everything that went before. They are looking for an angle on things, and the reason they often find one is that they not only know all the facts about their subject, but they also combine that knowledge with other apparently unconnected phenomena. Creativity is often a synthesis, bringing together two or more ideas to form a completely unique one.

'Thinking outside the box' is an interesting phrase that's become popular in business over recent years. It reflects the search for new ideas, a new angle, a unique approach. It's also a phrase that I know can throw some people into a silent panic: it demands that we come up with something new, and do it now. Where do you start?

But 'thinking outside the box' when viewed as a creative process has a very definite place to start. It begins with summarising the ideas that are already there. Then it takes into consideration other related facts and combines them.

Let's take an example:

1) Some humans love cats as much as they love people
2) Humans like to communicate using speech
3) Communication is a two-way process

Once I put these ideas together, I end up with a talking cat where before none existed. You might argue that this is a silly idea, that it doesn't solve any real problem. Here are several 'problems' that a talking cat could be an answer to:

How do I sell more cat food?

How do I teach young children how to look after cats?

How do I introduce a funny theme into a comedy series about witches?

How can I narrate my story about a lonely old man in a bed-sit, when there is no other human to observe him?

The point is that although the idea of talking cats has become quite commonplace, it was originally a unique synthesis of ideas (and probably goes back millennia, beyond Aesop's Fables).

Thought is the Mother of Invention. Once the idea exists, visualisation (i.e. imagination) is used to give the vision detail, and experiment is used to bring it into existence.

There are also short-term personal benefits to 'being creative'. Psychologists who have studied creativity have discovered that there is a feeling of 'flow' that creative individuals experience when they are performing at their best. When a person is 'in flow' it is similar to when an athlete is 'in the zone': everything is working as it should and at its peak; there's no sense of struggle, only complete concentration and absorption in the task. Our sense of time becomes distorted as we lose part of ourselves in the creative process.

This can give tremendous feelings of fulfilment, happiness and success. The state of 'flow' in and of itself is beneficial. And because it needs attention to and concentration on the task in hand, it's usually also rewarded by a great end-product, whether that's a new world record, or a new way to solve a problem.

The creative process can be applied to many different issues. Nowhere is it more useful than in the creative project of our own lives. Exactly the same process is at work in inventing and reinventing ourselves. We have memories that we can call on, and throughout this book we have urged you to call upon positive images from your past so that you can start to make your future. You also have thoughts and ideas of things not experienced — you can *imagine* positive experiences if you have none to call on. We've encouraged you to use all of your senses to bring details of those visualisations to mind, so that qualities of colour, sound, touch, taste and smell have been used to create mental images of a new, energetic version of your life. This is the most important creative task you have — to constantly reinvent yourself.

The next step is to think about all of your talents. What are you good at? What do you enjoy? How would you like to live? Don't discount anything, no matter how seemingly insignificant. Combine those ideas, and bring to mind that powerful picture of your future, successful self. Your imagination has the key to bringing about your desired future through the talents you have right now.

Be bold; be creative; take energetic action today.

Chapter 48
Ambition

Ambition is one of the great psychic energy producers, and it's also one of the most misunderstood. The key to ambition is to be the best possible version of yourself that you can be. This means that whatever you want to achieve in the external world is secondary — it's the internal development of your own character and thought that's important and that will guarantee success and fulfilment. Then the task becomes one of aligning your own internal truth with your objectives. This is the royal road to happiness. Discover what it is that you enjoy doing and are good at — then focus on that. As Alan Weiss says, one way or another, doing what you love will make you rich.

The truth is that you are creating your future right now, as you live and breathe and read this book. But what about your behaviour in general? Is it getting you where you want to be? If the answer is no, there's a good likelihood that it's because you are not doing whatever it is that makes you happy and what you excel at.

This is a sobering — and yet inspiring — thought, and it's good to take a moment or two to really let it sink in. *What you are thinking and doing today is creating your future.* Really understanding and acting on this puts you in control. It means that where you are today is the product of what you have done in the past. So start to act now to produce the tomorrow that you desire.

If it's true that thinking will bring about your reality, it must also be true that when you think big, ambitious thoughts, you'll bring a big ambitious reality into the world. The subconscious will act on what you tell it to do. If you feed it with small plans and dreams, it will guide your behaviour to realise those dreams. But if you think big thoughts, it will act in just the same way — the subconscious isn't phased by your ambition in the slightest.

Your conscious mind is a different story. If you hold fear there, it will transmit itself to the sub-conscious. Fear can hold back ambition more completely than anything else. If you can banish fear, you can allow yourself to think big thoughts and do big things.

It may be that your ambitions concern money. Until we are financially secure (remember that the definition of security differs for each person), it is difficult to move on to bigger and better things. This area of financial ambition is one that is often polluted by fear. A great and largely forgotten master of these issues who wrote in the early part of the Twentieth Century was Charles F. Haanel. This is what he had to say about the Laws of Abundance and Attraction:

"Fear is just the opposite from money consciousness; it is poverty consciousness; and as the law is unchangeable we get exactly what we give; if we fear, we get what is feared...

We make money by making friends, and we enlarge our circle of friends by making money for them, by helping them, by being of service to them. The first law of success then is service, and this in turn is built upon integrity and justice.

You can make a money magnet of yourself, but to do so you must first consider how you can make money for other people. If you have the necessary insight to perceive and utilize opportunities and propitious conditions and recognise values, you can put yourself in position to take advantage of them, but your greatest success will come as you are enabled to assist others."

You can use the ACE HIGH system to work on your ambitions. Those two words will remind you to think big and abandon fear. Bring your attention to what it is you want to achieve, and then concentrate on how to bring it about. Then formalise your goals, writing down exactly what it is you want to achieve. It's important at this stage though that you don't have your eyes set so firmly on the destination that you forget about the wonderful journey that you're on. Every day, invest your actions with massive energy to make progress, and make sure your health is looked after so you can enjoy everything that you do.

You need to be flexible when you're ambitious; the goals you set for yourself will have a tendency to transform into something else unexpectedly. It's then you will have to use your intelligence to readjust the course you are on.

Making these adjustments isn't failure, it is life.

Of course, even with adjustments made you'll run into the inevitable difficulties that challenge your endurance; and this is the time for gumption: determination, lightness of touch, a refusal to be done down. Finally, if you have an holistic attitude to your ambitions, they will be aligned to your values, and they in turn will ensure that success for you is success for those around you, your environment, even the planet itself.

Ambition is the harmonisation of all these factors. It's not a bloody fight to survive with tooth and nail; it's the way in which we bring together all of our skills, aptitudes and dreams to make our mark, to contribute fully whatever we have to give. And as Haanel often repeated, the more you give, the more you get.

Chapter 49
Adopt an alter-ego

This chapter is a lot of fun and a massive energy booster! What we are going to advise is that you pretend you are someone else...

No, we're not asking you to abandon your principles by taking on someone else's values; or to make a fool of your self; or suggesting that you aren't absolutely perfect as you are.

What we're doing is inviting you to try something that will give you a remarkable new take on the world, will help you to overcome shyness, lack of self-confidence or other fears, or let you experience as closely as possible what it's like to be someone else so that you can understand their point of view or how they came to be successful.

There's couple of different ways that you can do this. One of them is very simple indeed and can be done in a trice, so let's look at that first.

It's a sad fact that many people have a distorted mental image of their own appearance. One of the pioneers of thought-led personal development, Dr. Maxwell Maltz, the founder of Psycho-Cybernetics, was originally a pioneer plastic surgeon. As the doctor progressed in the field, he noticed that the results of the surgery he carried out on his patients had unpredictable results with regard to their self-esteem. Some people became much more confident and secure once their physical 'defect' was taken away; but many others did not experience any satisfaction from their new appearance, and issues of self-confidence, shyness and so on continued to plague them. Eventually, Dr Maltz found that working directly on the patients' self-esteem and the way they thought about themselves was more successful than surgery! It is the Self-Image, Dr. Maltz concluded, that is really in need of change.

So let's put all that a different way and try to take a short cut to a new self-image. If you are going to have a distorted self-image, why not try distorting it in your own favour for a day? Who is the most handsome / beautiful and charming person of your gender? You know, the one who you just know can handle any social situation successfully, with grace and charisma. Well, just for the day — that's you.

What would that feel like, to have the body of that person who is confident and attractive (by the way, this isn't just about physical attractiveness. Maybe you'd like to imagine what it's like to be Winston Churchill so you can be decisive, fearless and steadfast for the day!). How would you move? What would you say? How would your actions be different? Get into character, have fun, play the part. Try it!

Let's suppose you try it and you're successful. You may have been laughing inwardly at yourself at first at how 'silly' you were being. But then you start to really enjoy the game and get involved in it. You realise you're calling on resources that you never knew you had, maybe the same ones that great actors call on when they play a character unlike their own. Your speech and movements start to flow; as you play this new character, it turns out that you're more like you than the 'real' you is like you! Somehow, in the midst of acting like someone else, you find that you are at your most authentic.

Then you get home, look in the mirror, and the same old you looks back. What you have just proven to yourself is that your success is nothing to do with your appearance; it's all about drawing on the resources you have at your disposal and letting them flow naturally.

Please try this, especially if you have problems related to a lack of self-esteem, confidence or self-belief. What have you to lose?

Now for something that takes a little more than just your imagination. It's a technique called modelling that's been made popular by people who use NLP techniques.

This time, think about a person whose behaviour you want

to model. The idea is that it is our behaviour that produces our results, and our thoughts that produce our behaviour. So find out everything that you can about the person you want to model, and you will be able to behave like them and therefore produce similar results.

What you're trying to do is reproduce the physical and mental state of the person you are modelling. It isn't enough to simply understand what results that person achieves and how they appear to behave: you need more detail than that. You must reproduce everything possible about their physical and mental states.

For instance, if you were modelling a successful artist, you would want to know about their values and belief systems. How do they look at the world, and how do they see themselves in it? Are they confident about their abilities, bold and serious? Playful? Uncertain?

What kinds of thoughts do they have while preparing for and executing their works? Michelangelo would look at a block of marble and see the angel already there in it; then he would simply chip away to reveal it. That was Michelangelo's strategy. What is the strategy of the person you wish to model?

What is the physiology like of the person you are modelling? How do they breathe—deeply and slowly, or quickly and with shallow breaths? Do they stoop or stand tall, pace frantically or sit quiet?

This kind of modelling is less dependent on your own imagination, but can be more accurate if you want to produce the same kinds of results that your subject does. How about modelling someone you know who seems to have abundant energy? This could soon be you!

Chapter 50
Reject conformity!

One of the greatest energy sappers there is happens when a person feels trapped — trapped inside the expectations of others, spoken and unspoken social pressures, the demands of the family. The weight of conformity bears down on us from an early age. Some of us are taught not to stand out in the crowd, to be seen and not heard, and that it's vain, boastful and rude to shine the light of our talent where it might embarrass others.

So we learn to be like the rest. That's how we get accepted by the rest. We learn to look like one another, to act like clones, to know our places in the hierarchy. We learn to hold our tongues when our souls scream out that we should speak, or we play for cheap laughs and the acclaim of the ignorant. We accept what is not good enough for us, and we reject what would most allow us to be ourselves. We are like butterflies stuck in the pupal stage, limbless, soulless and brainless, forever frozen in waiting for the day when wings will grow.

No more.

Carpe Diem! *Seize* the day! *To thine own self be true!*

This is not about childish non-conformity, where the aim is to be the centre of attention. Real non-conformity is about courage, conviction and energy.

The other day Brian rode on the London tube and listened, amused, to two groups of boys, out for the day during the holidays. One group consisted of some young teenage middle-class white boys, and the other of slightly older black kids. Brian followed the two strands of conversation. One was about what subjects the boys would study at University after they left school. Brian heard a very plummy accent declare that he would probably become a lawyer, though his father favoured medicine.

The other conversation was about who the best rap band was at the moment. It was the amazing accent that caught Brian's attention — one that didn't exist thirty years ago, a mix of Cockney and Jamaican patois, rhyming slang with cool rhythms.

Of course, when Brian looked up, he realised that it was the white kids who were the rappers, and the black boys who were discussing education and the law. He had pigeon-holed them, put them in boxes, decided who they were. If enough people do that to them, maybe they *will* become the people in the box that we assign them to. Or perhaps they will refuse to conform, plough their own furrows, and make a difference to the world.

It isn't the act of non-conformity itself that makes a difference. It's the strength of character of those who walk their own path. This marks them out as exceptional people, and if they are strong enough to resist the pressures to be like just like everyone else, they will go on to do exceptional deeds. Not necessarily famous actions, but actions that count, that make a stand for individuality, courage and freedom.

The question of fame is an interesting one. Many non-conformists have fame — sometimes only on a fairly local scale, it's true — and then reject it because it threatens to tear down their principles. Instead of playing to the gallery and reaping the benefits of a spurious fame, they follow their hearts and sometimes slip into obscurity. But who knows what will happen to the work of such people. They burn with an inner fire, and their work will perhaps be appreciated by future generations.

Another species of non-conformist is the 'eccentric'. 'Eccentrics' are people who may have attracted that label because name-calling eases the embarrassment of the rest of us, who are terribly uncomfortable with any signs of originality or difference. They are often people who are socially awkward, have a disturbing tendency to speak the truth at inappropriate moments, and who find it hard to make the fine distinctions sometimes needed to negotiate the social niceties. The other kind of eccentric is the attention seeker who substitutes a flamboyant manner for a lack of talent.

Throughout this book we have encouraged you to go out and greet the world with energy and enthusiasm. This will take courage. It will make you stand out. It means that when someone asks you how you are, you won't be replying "mustn't grumble": you'll be replying with the truth. When there is a difficult task to do and a volunteer has been asked for — you'll be the one stepping forward, not for praise, not for glory, but because you have energy and commitment. Others will notice and they may well ostracise you.

If you find the thought of social isolation scary, take heart. When you have the courage of your convictions, you will attract the courageous, as well as those who want to learn your secret; when you have strength of character, you'll attract the strong; when you have the fearlessness to stand alone, you will soon enough have the company of heroes. Your band of friends may be smaller, but they will also be truer. If you lack arrogance and yet can still be independent of the good opinions of others, you will find your own way with energy and conviction, and you'll be joined by like minded spirits.

All the energy you need is inside you.

Believe in yourself; stand your ground; make your mark.

Chapter 51
Your energy profile

By the time we reach adulthood, we all have a particular energy disposition. But as they say, *it's not the hand you're dealt with, it's how you play it* that counts. So self-knowledge is important as you consider what you can do as an individual to change your energy profile for the best. You are the raw material that we have to work on — let's find out what you're made of!

To help you discover your energy profile, simply respond to the statements below. There's no need to agonise over each statement — just use your gut reaction as to whether you agree or disagree. Every response you give is on a scale where 1=Low and 5=High. So for instance, if the statement is 'On a Monday morning I feel totally energised", and you are bursting to start a new week with enthusiasm, commitment and joy, then you agree wholeheartedly and should score five. If you'd rather stay in bed and not bother, score 1 because you completely disagree.

The aim of the energy profile is to get you thinking about yourself, and to reveal which areas of your life really need some special energy attention. We're also trying to uncover *why* you lack (or are abundant in) energy in a certain area, so that you take actions that deal with the cause and not just the effect.

So for example, you may feel drained of energy by your tendency to procrastinate. But when you look a little deeper, you realise that the reason you are not getting on with things is that you lack self-confidence: you doubt your own ability to be successful, and even attempting a task that you may fail to complete makes you feel vulnerable. So in that example, what you would need to work on is your self-confidence. Look at our advice on what you can do to boost your energy, but remember that you are the world's foremost expert on yourself. Using the results of your energy profile, concentrate on finding what *you* can change to lead the most energetic life imaginable.

1. I can concentrate for long stretches of time without allowing myself to be distracted
   Disagree 1 2 3 4 5 Agree
2. I enjoy visualising the future
   Disagree 1 2 3 4 5 Agree
3. I eat healthily
   Disagree 1 2 3 4 5 Agree
4. I love being with friends more than I love solitude
   Disagree 1 2 3 4 5 Agree
5. I hold very strong beliefs
   Disagree 1 2 3 4 5 Agree
6. I love to discover new ideas
   Disagree 1 2 3 4 5 Agree
7. I use stories to make my point when I talk to people
   Disagree 1 2 3 4 5 Agree
8. I'm full of physical energy
   Disagree 1 2 3 4 5 Agree
9. I am never lonely
   Disagree 1 2 3 4 5 Agree
10. Values are important to me
    Disagree 1 2 3 4 5 Agree
11. Acquiring new knowledge is exciting
    Disagree 1 2 3 4 5 Agree
12. I love to make up stories in my head
    Disagree 1 2 3 4 5 Agree
13. I never have trouble getting out of bed in the morning
    Disagree 1 2 3 4 5 Agree
14. I don't wait to be asked to join in with a fun activity
    Disagree 1 2 3 4 5 Agree
15. I never procrastinate
    Disagree 1 2 3 4 5 Agree

16. Acquiring new skills is exciting

    Disagree   1   2   3   4   5   Agree

17. I often imagine looking more successful and healthy

    Disagree   1   2   3   4   5   Agree

18. I exercise at least three times a week

    Disagree   1   2   3   4   5   Agree

19. I'm the life and soul of the party

    Disagree   1   2   3   4   5   Agree

20. It's nice to be liked, but not necessary

    Disagree   1   2   3   4   5   Agree

21. I like to keep my mind razor sharp

    Disagree   1   2   3   4   5   Agree

22. I often imagine myself in new situations, with new people

    Disagree   1   2   3   4   5   Agree

23. Physical activity is one of my favourite things

    Disagree   1   2   3   4   5   Agree

24. I like to organise fun activities that involve my friends

    Disagree   1   2   3   4   5   Agree

25. I'm very self-confident in most situations

    Disagree   1   2   3   4   5   Agree

26. I'm always reading at least one book

    Disagree   1   2   3   4   5   Agree

27. I love to read fiction.

    Disagree   1   2   3   4   5   Agree

28. I don't like being a couch potato

    Disagree   1   2   3   4   5   Agree

29. Most people like me immediately

    Disagree   1   2   3   4   5   Agree

30. What people think of me is unimportant

    Disagree   1   2   3   4   5   Agree

31. I'd rather have an original, useful idea than a new car

    Disagree   1   2   3   4   5   Agree

32. When I listen to good music, I feel inspired

    Disagree   1   2   3   4   5   Agree

33. My friends often ask me where I get my energy from
    Disagree   1   2   3   4   5   Agree
34. I respect the beliefs of others
    Disagree   1   2   3   4   5   Agree
35. By my own standards, I am very successful
    Disagree   1   2   3   4   5   Agree
36. I would like to be known for my ideas rather than any other part of my character
    Disagree   1   2   3   4   5   Agree
37. My friends think I am creative
    Disagree   1   2   3   4   5   Agree
38. I recover quickly from a lack of sleep
    Disagree   1   2   3   4   5   Agree
39. I am sensitive to the feelings of others
    Disagree   1   2   3   4   5   Agree
40. I am unconventional
    Disagree   1   2   3   4   5   Agree
41. People admire my intellect
    Disagree   1   2   3   4   5   Agree
42. I am a creative person
    Disagree   1   2   3   4   5   Agree
43. My body weight is just about perfect
    Disagree   1   2   3   4   5   Agree
44. I encourage shy people to join in the fun
    Disagree   1   2   3   4   5   Agree
45. I know what motivates me
    Disagree   1   2   3   4   5   Agree
46. I have a powerful intellect
    Disagree   1   2   3   4   5   Agree
47. I'm always coming up with new ideas
    Disagree   1   2   3   4   5   Agree
48. I am very fit and healthy
    Disagree   1   2   3   4   5   Agree

49. Love is important to me
   Disagree   1   2   3   4   5   Agree
50. I know what my purpose is
   Disagree   1   2   3   4   5   Agree

Your scores!

Intellectual Energy

Add up the scores to questions 1, 6, 11, 16, 21, 26, 31, 36, 41 and 46

10—20

You have very low intellectual energy. This may be because you have bags of emotional energy to compensate (see your scores for emotional energy. If they too are very low, unfortunately, you may be asleep!). Without looking into new ideas, you are unlikely to come up with any of your own. You are missing out greatly on one of the great spices of life!

It's also possible that you under-rate your own intellectual capabilities. Remember a time when your thinking has produced a new way of doing things, even if it's only a minor achievement. Then use that memory to motivate your thinking in the future. Most of all though, you should develop your powers of concentration. This needs practice and application. Take a subject you are interested in, and resolve to become an expert in it.

21—30

Your intellectual energy is quite low, but may be balanced by scores in other areas. Work on improving your concentration, and realise that without new knowledge, new ideas are more difficult to generate, and ideas are the engines of change. If you want to change, you must sharpen your concentration, and practise applying your knowledge in practical situations at every opportunity.

31—40
You have good intellectual energy, and have a very healthy love of thinking and new ideas. The knowledge you acquire through your intellectual pursuits will enable you to remain flexible, skilled and interesting, and you will be able to adapt to shifting circumstances.

41—50
For you, ideas aren't work — they're play. Your love of intellectual pursuits and new ideas will always mean that you are interesting and adaptable to change. You may be — *or will be* — a great inventor, artist or philosopher, depending on your other results.

It's possible that your love for the life of the mind makes you seem like a cold fish, so you may need to work on your emotional intelligence. Your self-confidence when it comes to ideas may not be reflected by your confidence in social situations.

Creative Energy
Add up the scores to questions 2, 7, 12, 17, 22, 27, 32, 37, 42 and 47

10—20
You are not using two of the most powerful tools at your disposal — the imagination in general and visualisation in particular. Use the imagination to bring the future you want into existence... otherwise you will end up with the future you *don't* want. Then use visualisation to fill in the details of exactly how things will be. Remember, creative use of the imagination isn't all just about the future either, it's about living a wonderful life today. Read this book again — properly this time!

21—30
Your creative energy is quite low. Work back through the book

practising the suggestions in each chapter for a week at a time. Be aware that this isn't just about 'artistic' creativity — it's about creating the future for yourself that you want.

Before you use visualisation techniques, always find some meditative silence first. You need to be calm, quiet and comfortable when you are preparing to get the creative juices flowing.

31—40

You have good creative energy, and you're well on your way to bringing the life you want into existence. Have confidence in your ability to do so, as creating your own life is the most important act of the imagination that anyone can do.

Make sure that you're in a profession or walk of life where you have an outlet for your artistic and creative energies — if not, frustration will result.

41—50

You are imaginative, creative and artistic. You see your own life for the work of art that it is — something entirely under your control, like a painter's canvas. It's important that you don't hide your light under a bushel — find a worthy outlet for your imagination that will make a difference in the world.

It's hard to find any words of caution for the truly imaginative, other than to say that you should be sure to marry your creative abilities to your values and beliefs, so you may need to work on your Personal Energy score.

Physical Energy

Add up the scores to questions 3, 8, 13, 18, 23, 28, 33, 38, 43 and 48

10—20

You have very low levels of physical energy. This could be due to some physical problem, but is more likely a combination of that with a lack of self-confidence, and some serious setback you have had in life. Remember, the body doesn't exist in a vacuum, it's an integral part of a system that includes your mind and soul.

You need to work on all aspects of your energy, because they all effect physical wellbeing. A big boost in one area could be just the thing you need to make you feel more energised physically. Get the best exercise and dietary advice that you can, and go back and do all of the exercises in this book — a chapter at a time, one a week!

21—30

Your energy levels really need a boost. More than any other area, your physical energy is dependent on your energy as a whole, so look at your life to see what is out of kilter, and work on bringing balance into everything you do. Use visualisation exercises to imagine yourself healthier, brighter and more energetic. That is the first step to priming your subconscious so that it works to give you a boost.

Quality rest and nutrition are next in line. Think of every piece of food and drink that enters your body today as forming your body — and its energy levels — tomorrow. In parallel, think about finding a form of exercise that you enjoy and that you can do regularly. Slowly but surely your energy will increase. To accelerate the process, tell yourself, right now, that you are already full of energy. Bring that thought to mind powerfully and often.

31—40

You have an excellent basis of fitness and health. It may be that you could feel even healthier and fitter if you were a little more consistent in your exercise and eating habits. Remember too that you have a right to feel as good as you can. Don't allow other people to project their guilt about their poor physical condition onto you. Build your health and fitness regime into your life. If family and friends occasionally have to take a backseat, that's ok. They will get far more from your friendship and care when you are fit, healthy and happy.

41—50

You are bouncing with physical energy and in the best of health—and everyone knows it. Use this blessing as a foundation for all of the other areas in your life where you want to succeed. Physical fitness is one more barrier that you don't have to overcome. Now you just have to put it to good use to achieve everything you want in life.

Emotional Energy

Add up the scores to questions 4, 9, 14, 19, 24, 29, 34, 39, 44, 49

10—20

I'm afraid I have some bad news for you—you're an Energy Vampire! When people are around you, they tend to feel deflated, uncomfortable and irritable.

But you, my friend, have as much a right to happiness as anyone else on this earth. Who knows how you came to be the way you are? Perhaps you were undervalued, ignored, even mistreated as a child or as a young adult. And now, you either find it very painful to overcome your shyness, mix socially and *be* yourself, or you find it hard not to keep your critical thoughts and behaviour *to* yourself, and like to be the centre of attention in a way that makes people wish they were somewhere else.

There are some simple things you can do, all of which have been written about at greater length in other chapters. The two most important things to do are these: first, let go of whatever and whoever hurt you in the past; second, always remember that you get back what you give out. Try giving out some love, peace and understanding and that's exactly what you will receive.

21—30
Your emotional energy is low. The best advice we can give you is to learn to love and value yourself. You have as much right to happiness as anyone else, and it is just out there waiting for you. You don't have to have a smile plastered on your face for twenty four hours a day, and you don't need to be the life and soul of the party. You just need to recognise your own worth, and quietly go about life making sure that you use all your talents to the best of your abilities. Be true to yourself and others will sense that you are genuine... and will give their emotional energy to you in bucket loads.

31—40
You have a well-balanced personality that respects and is sensitive to the needs of people, but doesn't cross the line into unwanted interference in the lives of others. Don't be scared of being unconventional sometimes—if that is what is required. Use your ability to get on well with people to help both them and you.

41—50
You are a larger than life character who gets noticed. You are also part of a tiny percentage of the population, because people who are both socially extrovert and very sensitive to the needs and feelings of others are rare. Either that, or you have a twisted view of yourself! Carry on enjoying life, giving pleasure to others and taking happiness where you can find it.

Personal Energy
Add up the scores to questions 5, 10, 15, 20, 25, 30, 35, 40, 45 and 50

10—20
It's likely that you have several areas of your life where you are

underperforming. There are several issues with your outlook on life, all of which are making each other worse. It's a vicious circle—your lack of direction in life is leading to a lack of self-confidence, and that is causing you to not develop the strong values and beliefs that you need to develop motivation and direction.

The good news is that improvement in one of these areas will have a knock-on effect on the others. Soon, with a little will-power, gumption and above all visualisation, you can be in a positive feedback situation where things quickly get better.

21—30

Make it your mission to get things done. Realise that the reason you aren't getting things done is due to your own lack of self-confidence. So before you undertake something that you have been avoiding like the plague, visualise a past success. Amplify that image of your successful self in every way—make it brighter, more colourful, more beautiful. That is the capable you—the you who is going to take the next difficult thing that comes along by the scruff of the neck. Build on it—one success at a time.

31—40

You're self-confident, successful and motivated. You seem to have a superb moral balance in your life between what is important internally and externally. You know what you want and you are going to get it, but would probably be horrified to get success at someone else's expense. You have strong values that will help you to make decisions instinctively, and without regret.

41—50

Your self-confidence and independence from others is frightening. This can bring you great success or great unhappiness, and the reason is very simple. Your single mindedness can come across as inflexibility; your self-confidence as arrogance; and your self-reliance as contempt. You are a Nietzschean Superman or Superwoman, but that involves danger as well as exhilaration. You can be a force for great good, or great evil.

Overall Energy Profile
Add up the scores for all questions.

50—100 Vampire
You need to get your pulse checked! Seriously though, you are missing out on all the fun and zest in life, and what's more, your effect on other people will make it difficult for you to get help. Nevertheless, you do need some help, and we recommend that you visit our website at www.zingzip.com to see a range of options you can consider. Do it right now!

101—150 Snoozer
Go over the exercises in this book and boost yourself up to an Energy Angel. Identify the area(s) where you need more energy and focus on just one of them. You may find that improving one part of the overall picture also improves everything else. Remember ACE HIGH—focus your Attention on what you want in your life and it will manifest itself; Concentrate on what you want to achieve and it will happen; act with massive Energy to bring it about; get your Health right to support your new activities; develop and use your Intelligence to make finer distinctions about your goals; when the going gets tough, the tough use Gumption; and finally, make sure your Holistic attitude checks that your goals are aligned with your values.

151—200 Angel
You are not only full of energy—you know that the secret to gaining energy is to give it out. That attracts more energy to

you because energetic people want to be with you. You are well balanced, fun, intelligent, but with a hint of inner steel that will get you to where you want to be.

201—250 Junkie

You are so fired up that you make the rest of us look lazy. The problem is, your attitude can appear to be overbearing due to your absolute concentration on being the best that you can be. Although it's true that you can never have too much energy, make sure that the things you're driven to achieve are really important life goals, and take care not to drive yourself and others to the point where something breaks.

Chapter 52
Write your own chapter!

A life coach always tries to think of every relevant question to ask a client, to lead them to what action needs to be taken. Sometimes, despite the best efforts of the coach and client, there's still something left unsaid, something left under a stone somewhere, undiscovered. And yet, the client can't bring herself to tell the coach what that something is — she'd like them to ask *her* the question.

In the life coaching world there's a way round this problem. The coach can ask the client: *What is the question that I have not asked you?*

Usually the client knows exactly what question they wish they had been asked. They ask it themselves, out loud, and immediately start to deal with the real issues. It soon becomes clear what action needs to be taken.

So, given everything I've just said, *what chapter haven't we written for you?*

What's your own master key to open the vault of energy?

Do you have something you could build into your daily routine that would energise, motivate and send you out with a bounce in your step every single day? Perhaps it's a physical exercise that leaves you feeling relaxed and alert, or a food or drink that drives you out into the big bad world with a never say die attitude. Maybe you have thought of an affirmation that is powerful enough to convince the deepest part of you that you have energy to burn. Your own words are the most powerful for you: we don't know what they are, but you can find them yourself.

There are many different ways to set goals, and many can be successful. We are all so different in the things that resonate with us: find your own inspiring way to set goals that will energise you.

You know yourself better than anyone else ever can. You know what moves you, inspires you, impassions you.

Your energy is particular to you, too. Perhaps you have times of the day when you're at your best and others where you sag. We don't understand this 'graveyard shift' thing that trainers talk about, where they seem to expect people to fall asleep after lunch. But if that applies to you, plan around it. Be daring — skip lunch! Work all night and rest all day, if necessary. Do what works for you.

What is obvious to us may be obscure to you, and vice versa. Perhaps there is something screaming out to you, that you just know is the key to huge bursts of energy — and yet it isn't here in these pages. Go for it! Do it!

Finally, we hope you have enjoyed the book and feel massively energised. If you read it cover to cover, great! But you can go back and dip into it when you need a boost, a technique to get you back on track. Another way to use the book is to go back and read one chapter a week, and really concentrate on perfecting each technique, or on putting the principles into practice. Some of the advice we've given here is deceptively simple, and it takes practice and repetition to get the best possible benefits.

Good luck in your search for energy! Never forget that it's inside you and all around you, waiting for your command.

Zingzip today!

For more inspiration and motivation
as well as further ways
to fire up your life
visit
www.zingzip.com

ISBN 1412084468